THE STORY OF
STEVIE
WONDER

THE STORY OF
STEVIE WONDER

JAMES HASKINS

Illustrated with photographs

Lothrop, Lee & Shepard Company
A Division of William Morrow and Co., Inc. / New York

1   2   3   4   5   80   79   78   77   76
Library of Congress Cataloging in Publication Data
Haskins, James (date)
    The story of Stevie Wonder.
    SUMMARY: A biography of the blind composer, pianist, and
singer who was a child prodigy and went on to win ten Grammy
awards.
    1. Wonder, Stevie—Juvenile literature. [1. Wonder, Stevie.
2. Musicians. 3. Negroes—Biography] I. Title.
ML3930.W65H4   784'.092'4 [B] [92]   75-37517
ISBN 0-688-41740-X   ISBN 0-688-51740-4 lib. bdg.

Grateful acknowledgment is made to reprint material as follows:

Lyrics from "Heaven Is Ten Zillion Light Years Away," "Living for the City," "All in Love Is Fair," "Higher Ground," and "You Haven't Done Nothin' " written by Stevie Wonder © 1973, 1974 by Jobete Music Co., Inc., and Black Bull Presentations, Inc. All rights reserved. Reprinted by permission.

Excerpts from "Growing Up Stevie Wonder" by O'Connell Driscoll © 1975 by Rolling Stone. All rights reserved. Reprinted by permission of *Rolling Stone Magazine*.

Excerpts from "Hey, Stevie Wonder, How's Your Bad Self?" by Burr Snider © 1974 by Esquire, Inc. Reprinted by permission of *Esquire Magazine*.

Excerpts from "A Sense of Wonder" by Jack Slater © 1975 by The New York Times Company. Reprinted by permission.

Excerpts from "Superstars of Soul" © 1975 by Penthouse Poster Press, Ltd. Reprinted by permission.

Excerpts from "Stevie, The Wonder Man" by Maureen Orth © 1974 by Newsweek, Inc. All rights reserved. Reprinted by permission.

The author wishes to thank the following people for helping to make this book possible: Karen Hodge and Joy Sato at Motown; Frank Benson and J. M. Stifle for their help in researching the book; Mary Ellen Arrington, who typed the manuscript; and Kathy Benson, without whom this book would not have been realized.

To Stevie Wonder,
in hopes that one day
his "fulfillingness" will be total.

Contents

WARTOKE CONCERN, INC.

1
Growing Up in a World of Darkness

"See, about sound . . . ," Stevie Wonder says, "there's one thing you gotta remember about sound—sound happens all the time, *all* the time. If you put your hands right up to your ears, if you close your eyes and move your hands back and forth, you can hear the sound getting closer and farther away. . . . Sound bounces off everything, there's always something happening."

Stevie Wonder was born Steveland Morris on May 13, 1950, in Saginaw, Michigan. He was the third boy in a family that would eventually include five boys and one girl. All except Stevie were born without handicaps. He was born prematurely, and his early birth led to his total blindness.

"I have a dislocated nerve in one eye and a cataract [a milky film] on the other," Stevie explains. "It may have happened from being in the incubator too long and receiving too much oxygen. You see, I was premature by one full month. But a girl who was born on the same day that I was was also put into the incubator, and she died. I personally think that I'm lucky to be alive."

Stevie had retrolental fibroplasia, which was indeed produced by too much oxygen in his incubator. At the time the role of oxygen in producing this kind of blindness had not been discovered. The condition is permanent and cannot be corrected.

Stevie has never seen, and never will see, a tree, a cloud, a butterfly, or the faces of people he loves. But, as he says, "In my mind I can see all these things in my own way, in the manner that we [blind people] can see them." A blind infant has ways of "seeing" the world around him through hearing and touch and inner feeling. In this way, Stevie could "see" his mother and sense her feelings.

Most parents of handicapped children feel great guilt. More deep-rooted than most people realize are religious and superstitious beliefs that sins or mistakes by parents are responsible for their children's handicaps. Stevie's mother did not feel guilty. But she was a religious person and felt that if a higher power had made Stevie blind, then perhaps this same higher power could make him see. This belief was encouraged by the various faith healers to whom she took Stevie. For them, blindness was a disease that could be healed. And so they prayed over Stevie, or touched his eyes, or shook his small body and shouted into his face in order to awaken the power of the Lord that was in him and that could make him well.

Stevie was too young at the time to understand what this was all about. Understanding came when he was about seven years old. A doctor explained that while others could see, he could not, and that this fact would make his life different from that of other little boys. When he was about two or three years old, he began to notice that he could not do certain things that others could do. For example, he seemed to bump into furniture and doors more than other people. When he began walking with his arms stretched out in front of him—so he would bump his hands rather than his head—his mother made him stop. But he did not realize he would never be able to walk about without danger of bumping into things. He just thought his brothers and his adult relatives were better at walking around because they were older than he was or grown up.

"I guess that I first became aware that I was blind," Stevie recalls "—and I just vaguely remember this— when I'd be wallowing around in the grass back of the house, and I'd get myself and my clothes soiled. My mother would get on me about that. She explained that I couldn't move about so much, that I'd have to try and stay in one place."

It was then that Stevie first began to realize he was

blind, although he did not really understand what it meant. His two older brothers, Calvin and Milton, who were also very young, didn't really understand it either. They thought, at first, that their little brother simply needed more light than other people did.

Their mother left them alone quite frequently, for she had to go out to work in order to support them, and could not afford a baby sitter. Left to themselves, the two older boys managed to get into quite a bit of mischief; and once the results of that mischief were nearly disastrous.

Stevie recalls, "I remember my brothers Milton and Calvin were messing around with a lot of stuff in the house, had stuff all over everywhere, jam and bubble gum and stuff . . . and they had a garbage can and some matches in the house, and they were saying, 'you know, Stevie needs some more light. Wonder what we can do to get him some light? Maybe we can set this thing . . . like start a fire in here and he'll have some more light.' So they went and started a fire and almost burned the house up."

Needless to say, all three boys got "whumped," as Stevie puts it, for that. He recalls getting "whumped" quite frequently, for like any little boy he got into his share of mischief. In a way, it was fortunate that his brothers were so close to him in age that when he was very young neither of them understood that because he was blind he was different. They understood that he could not see with his eyes, but he seemed to be able to "see" with his hands. They knew he could not play catch, but they saw no reason why he could not climb trees.

Stevie did indeed climb trees and, with a passenger to steer, ride a bicycle. He also joined his brothers in jumping from one woodshed roof to another! It seems hard to believe, but it is true. Stevie merely used his "sonar." This is the ability to locate an object by listening to the echo a sound makes as it bounces off it. Thus, Stevie had learned to call out and then listen to his call. If a woodshed rooftop was very close, his call would sound different than if the rooftop was farther away. Everyone who can hear has this same ability. But those who are sighted do not need to develop it. They can *see* how close or far away an object like a woodshed rooftop is. Blind children probably develop this ability at about one year of age.

They were just children together, the two who could see and the one who could not. They played together, they fought together, they were gullible together. "I think back to when we were little kids in Saginaw," Stevie recalls. "My father used to tell us that Saginaw was only twelve miles from the North Pole, and me and my brother Calvin used to go around telling people that we were born twelve miles from the North Pole. I believed that for a long time." Later on, Stevie's brother Calvin would be able to look at a globe or a map and understand how far away the North Pole was from Saginaw, Michigan. Stevie would be unable to do so.

"When I was young," he says, "my mother taught

me never to feel sorry for myself, because handicaps are really things to be used, another way to benefit yourself and others in the long run." This was the best possible advice Stevie's mother could have given. He learned to regard his blindness in more than one way. It could be a hindrance, but it could also be a special gift. He was able to accept this idea, sometimes better than his mother could.

"I know it used to worry my mother," Stevie recalls, "and I know she prayed for me to have sight someday, and so finally I just told her that I was *happy* being blind, and I thought it was a gift from God, and I think she felt better after that."

Stevie was a lucky child in many ways. He was lucky to have two brothers close enough to him in age not to understand at first about his blindness and to expect him to do many of the things they did. He was also lucky to have a mother and a father, and occasionally an uncle, who understood how important sound was to him, and how important it was for him to learn to identify things he could not see by their sound. He recalls:

"I remember people dropping money on the table and saying, 'What's that, Steve?' That's a dime—buh-duh-duh-da; that's a quarter—buh-duh-duh-duh-da; that's a nickel. I could almost always get it right except a penny and a nickel confused me.

"I don't really feel my hearing is any better than yours," Stevie says now; "we all have the same

14

abilities, you know. The only difference is how much you use it." Encouraged by his family, Stevie used his hearing more and more as he grew older. He learned how to tell birds apart by their call, and to tell trees apart by the sound their leaves made as they rustled in the wind. He learned to tell when people were tired or annoyed or pleased by listening to the tone of their voices. His world of sound grew larger and larger, and the most frightening experience for him was silence. He depended so on sound that silence, for him, was like total darkness for deaf children. It is hard for sighted and hearing people to understand this. Perhaps the best way to understand is to imagine being shut up in a dark, soundproof box. People need to feel that they are part of the world around them. It is hard enough to do so when one cannot see, or when one cannot hear; but it is doubly hard for a blind person in a silent room or a deaf person in total darkness.

Stevie also learned to use his memory. Sometimes it was his mental memory that helped him find an object. Sometimes it was his "muscle" memory that he used, especially in getting about the house in Saginaw. Sighted people use their muscle memory, too. If we walk around a room long enough and often enough, we can do so even in total darkness. It is like tying shoelaces. After tying our shoelaces hundreds of times, we do not have to think about what we are doing.

It was especially hard for Stevie, then, when his mother and father decided to move from Saginaw to the city of Detroit. The family moved into a house in the black section on the east side of the city. It meant a great deal of adjustment for Stevie—a whole new house to get used to, furniture in different places, strange new sounds, and much less freedom to move around. The out-of-doors was just as new, only more frightening because it was larger. He would have to find out all over again where the trees were, or what was a street and what was an alley. He did not know whether the people in the neighborhood would be friendly or hostile and suspicious.

At first Stevie's mother was afraid to let him go outside, even with his brothers, unless she was with them. She realized that Milton and Calvin were too young to be responsible for their younger brother. They were too likely to be attracted by something across the street, or only a few yards away. "We'll be right back, Stevie," they would say. But Stevie, suddenly all alone and unable to see where his brothers had gone, would be frightened. He would start out to find them, and there was no telling what he might bump into, or trip over, or get in the way of.

So, Stevie's mother kept him inside at first. There he was safer from real harm, but he still was not safe from bumping into things and hurting himself. Stevie was an energetic little boy; he needed to move around. He particularly needed to move around because his lack of sight deprived him of much of the outside stimulation sighted children receive. Yet, Stevie did not like to get hurt. For a while, before he had gotten used to the new house, he did a lot of jumping up and down. He knew the ceiling was too high for him to bump into, and he knew the floor was beneath him. It was a much safer activity than moving forward or backward or sideways.

He also spent a lot of time beating on things, to make sounds and to make music. Although his mother was a gospel singer, the family was not especially musical. But Stevie had shown musical interest and ability very young. By the time he was two years old his favorite toys were two spoons, with which he would beat rhythmically on pans and tabletops and anything else his mother would let him beat on. When she began to worry about her furniture, she bought him cardboard drums from the dime store. None of them lasted very long. "I'd beat 'em to death," Stevie says with a chuckle. But there would always be a new drum, and there were other toy instruments as well.

"One day someone gave me a harmonica to put on my key chain, a little four-hole harmonica," Stevie recalls. He managed to get a remarkable range of sounds from that toy instrument.

"Then one day my mother took me to a picnic and someone sat me behind my first set of drums. They put my foot on the pedal and I played. They gave me a quarter. I liked the sound of quarters."

At a very early age, too, Stevie began to sing. All

voices were very important to him, for they brought him closer to the world around him, a world he could not see. As he grew older, his own voice became particularly important to him, especially at night when the rest of the house was silent. He learned the endless possibilities of the human voice by experimenting with his own, and by mimicking others'.

Within a year or two after the move to Detroit, Milton, Calvin, and Stevie had a new baby brother, Larry. Stevie was fascinated by the sounds the baby made and quickly was able to identify their meaning.

Stevie's family encouraged his musical ability, for they understood how much making sounds and making music meant to him. They also realized he had talent, and they were pleased, for no one else in the family really had it, especially the ability to play musical instruments.

Many people believe that blind people have natural musical ability. This is not true. Blind people have no more natural musical talent than sighted people. Some blind people are "tone-deaf," just as some sighted people are. Also, black people have no more natural sense of rhythm than do people of other races. So the fact that Stevie Wonder was both black and blind did not give him his musical talent. And that musical talent would have made little difference in his life if he had not been encouraged to develop it.

Music itself, not necessarily made by him, became very important to him. He loved to listen to the radio; his earliest memory is of hearing Johnny Ace singing "Pledging My Love" on the radio. Shortly before he entered school he was given a small transistor radio for his very own. From then on, that radio was his constant companion. He even slept with it under his pillow at night. It played softly, providing sounds for him in an otherwise silent apartment. When he started school, he insisted on taking it to school with him.

Stevie was enrolled in special classes for the blind in the Detroit public school system. A special bus picked him up every morning and brought him back every afternoon. Stevie wished he could walk to school as his brothers did, and go to their neighborhood school. But he was learning to adjust to the fact that he must lead a different life, and in his special classes he was taught many things that would help him lead as normal a life as possible.

He learned to speak more clearly. Many blind children learn to talk at a later age than sighted children and they do not, at first, talk as well. This is natural. Learning to talk takes much effort, and it is especially hard for a child who lacks one of his senses. While learning to talk is hardest of all for a deaf child, it is difficult as well for a blind child. Children learn to talk by imitating people who can talk. Sighted children are able to imitate both the sounds people make and the way they move their lips to make them. Stevie could not see how other people shaped their lips to form the "o" sound, for example. He could not see how they put their tongue between their teeth to make the "th" sound. At school he was taught how to make those and other sounds more clearly.

He also learned to show on his face his feelings and moods. Facial expressions are instinctive to human beings. All babies smile and laugh and cry and show discomfort on their faces—even blind babies. But as time goes on, blind babies smile and frown less and less. This is because they cannot see smiles and frowns on the faces of others. Sighted babies begin to see that facial expressions have meaning, blind babies cannot. Sighted people do not like to see the "silent faces" of the blind, and those who teach blind children know it will be best for the children if they learn to show expression on their faces. That way they will be more like other people, and better accepted in the sighted world.

At school Stevie was also helped to increase his skill in using his sense of hearing in place of eyes. He had learned by himself how to make use of the echoes sounds make when they bounce off objects. He could jump from one woodshed roof to another by calling out and listening to the echo of his call, which told him how far away the next roof was. But he couldn't go through life shouting. At school he learned that by snapping his fingers, or listening to his own footsteps, he could find out the same thing. He learned to be more skilled in using his "sonar." He also learned to be more aware of "sound shadows." These are made when a large object masks, or blocks, the sound waves of passing objects. If one learns to listen for these sound shadows, he can sense when he is coming close to large trees, cars, poles, corners of buildings. With practice, he can figure out how large an object such as a building is, by measuring in his mind the beginning and ending of the sound shadow.

Stevie learned, too, to make better use of his sense of touch. He learned to feel the differences between wood and metal, to notice changes in the air in different parts of a room by feeling drafts on his skin. He learned how to feel the differences between grass and dirt and gravel and cement under his feet. And he was given things that were not in his home so that he could learn about them by touching them. Most blind children do not naturally develop their sense of touch and must be taught to do so. It is very important for them to develop sensitivity in this area, for it is how they will read. At school Stevie learned braille, the system of raised dots, each combination standing for a letter or sound, invented by Frenchman Louis Braille. He and his blind classmates learned to read by running their hands along rows of these raised dots, and they learned to write by typing on a braille typewriter. They also "read" books by listening to

21

records and tapes of books, but braille reading was stressed most strongly. It was hard to learn, but once learned it opened up new worlds for Stevie and his classmates, just as reading regular books opens up new worlds for sighted children. When Stevie had mastered braille, he was rewarded with a braille Bible.

"The sense of touch. I dig it," says Stevie. "It's a way of bringing the world closer to me. It helps me give off good vibes." Every day, practically, he learned something at school that made his world a little larger, and that made the outside world seem a little less strange and frightening.

Still, life was hard for Stevie. The older he grew the more he realized how different he was, how much he could not do that sighted children could. No matter how developed his sense of touch became, there were some things he could never understand through touch. He could never touch the sun, or the horizon. He could never touch a mountain. Some things were too fragile, like snowflakes and live butterflies. It would be too dangerous to try to understand burning or boiling through touch. No matter how developed his ability to measure "sound shadows" became, he would only be able to measure the width and bulk of a large building, not its height. He could learn that the sky is blue and the grass green, but he would never *see* blue or green. He could not *watch* television.

It was sometimes hard to get along with other children. Many of his classmates were partially sighted, and they considered themselves, even if they could only tell the difference between darkness and light, superior to the totally blind children. Others had not been born blind, but had lost their sight later. They could remember what people's faces looked like; they could remember colors. Often they reminded Stevie and the other children who had been blind from birth of this fact.

Sighted children attended the same school, and they often whispered about "the blind kids" as they passed by. Adults did the same thing. Somehow, normal people have the idea that blind people cannot hear them. It was hard to deal in an honest way with sighted people or even with his partially sighted classmates.

Being blind is to be exposed to constant frustrations. Dropping something, especially something small, means having to grope about with little chance of finding it. Some blind children won't even bother looking for an object they have dropped because they are embarrassed to be seen groping about for it.

Eating with a knife and fork takes time to learn. Sighted people do not realize how much they rely on their eyes when they eat food in this manner. For blind people, memory plays an important role in this activity. It is important to know the types and placement of food on the plate. The sense of smell also plays a part. A keen sense of smell, like very acute hearing, requires practice to develop. It is not something that blind people are born with. Once they do develop their sense of smell they can use it to identify objects, people (every person has a distinctive odor), and places. But it takes time and practice.

Many blind people, including Stevie, enjoy television and going to movies, but there are times when the dialogue does not explain the action, or when action is occurring and there is no dialogue at all to explain it. Blind people have to depend on a companion to serve as a narrator for them, which works fine sometimes. But sometimes the companion can get caught up in the story and forget to narrate. This is very frustrating for one who cannot see.

A blind person is not free, as a sighted person is, to jump up and run, or even hurry, somewhere. He cannot decide to go down to the store, or even across the street, without first thinking and planning the trip; and often it is necessary to find someone who has time and is willing to act as a guide.

The totally blind know that they must rely on sighted people to help them, and that is hard to adjust to. They resent the sighted for being able to see while they cannot. At the same time they are afraid to anger the sighted, for they need them too much. Often blind people are forced to smile and say thank you when what they really want to do is to strike out and hurt the sighted person who has helped them because he or she is one of the lucky ones.

Stevie had an additional problem in getting along

with other children. Not only was he blind; he was also black. At first it might seem that the idea of skin color should not be very important to a child who has never seen color. But blackness is not just skin color; it is a culture, a way of looking at things. People divide themselves into "Us" and "Them" because of skin color, but that is not the only division. We also divide ourselves because of religion, education, economic class. If everyone in the entire world were blind, people would still divide themselves into "Us" and "Them"; it just would not be on the basis of appearance.

In his early years, before he had entered school, Stevie had heard his parents talk about racial matters. He knew that he and his family were something called black, or Negro, although that didn't mean much to him. He also knew that some people whom his parents called whites were disliked and distrusted by his parents. They denied equal rights to Negroes, he heard: they kept them from getting jobs and houses in nice neighborhoods; they looked down their noses at Negroes.

At school Stevie heard other students call black people names. It seemed to him that the white kids were better off than he. They had fathers who were around much more than his, and who had better jobs. Stevie knew his family was quite poor.

"I wasn't aware of it as much as other kids would be," says Stevie. "Being blind, I didn't see the things

I didn't have, like on television, for example. So I was sort of lucky." But there were ways of knowing about poverty without having to see it.

"I remember," he says, "watching television and hearing, 'Get this Hostess Twinkie,' and kids smacking their lips and saying 'Oooh, it's good!' And I remember kids in school saying, 'Look what I got for Christmas!' It did make me wish I could have those things."

He could remember back in Saginaw, ". . . when I was younger, my mother, my brothers and I had to go on this drydock where there was coal and steal some to keep warm. To a poor person that is not stealing, that is not crime; it's a necessity."

Today Stevie, who enjoys mimicking voices, sometimes does the voice of a "little urban white kid," and undoubtedly it comes out of his own past: "My dad makes twenty-five hundred dollars a week. He gets us all the things you could ever want to eat. Our pantry is stacked with food, man. We're *never* hungry."

At home, Stevie heard his brothers and their friends talk about the white kids they knew. Before long, even though Stevie could not himself see color, he was very aware of skin color, and in addition to being self-conscious because of his blindness he was a little bit ashamed of being black.

"I remember when I was little," says Stevie, "I used to listen to this black radio station in Detroit on my way to school. Like I was the only black kid on the bus, and I would always turn the radio down, because I felt ashamed to let them hear me listening to B.B. King. But I *loved* B.B. King. Yet I felt ashamed because—because I was *different* enough to want to hear him and because I had never heard him anywhere else."

True, the "rhythm and blues" style of B.B. King, now a well-known entertainer, was quite new at the time, and most kids do not want to risk being made fun of by their friends for liking something different from what their friends like. Stevie, of course, had the added problem of being a blind kid and, on the school bus, the only black kid. But he was not about to stop listening to B.B. King; he simply played his radio softly in situations where he felt uncomfortable. That radio meant more to him than just about anything else in the world.

"I spent a lot of time listening to the radio," Stevie recalls, "and I was able to relate to the different instruments and know what they were. I began to know them by name. I used to listen to this program on station WCHB . . . called 'Sundown.' The disc jockey was named Larry Dixon and he always played a lot of old songs. There was one thing he played, it was his theme song . . . da da duh duh *dommm* da duh . . . da da da da *dommm dommm* da da duh. . . . Oh, it's really a bad tune, really a beautiful song—can't think of the name right now, but I could never forget that tune."

27

Stevie Wonder welcomes sound, for it is what brings the world to him. A radio is rarely far from his side. His hearing is so acute that even in a crowded room, he can isolate a single conversation. WARTOKE CONCERN, INC.

Remembering all those hours of listening, all those exciting sounds that came out of his radio, Stevie gets excited even today:

"The kind of stuff I used to listen to was like . . . oh, like 'Dream Lover,' you know, and some Mary Wells stuff, 'On Broadway,' stuff like that. I liked the Five Royales, Johnny Ace, Clyde McPhatter, Jackie Wilson, Jimmy Reed, the Drifters. Oh, Jimmy Reed. Oh, I used to love that boy, I swear. Oh the music! Jumping around and dancing . . . do you remember that tune, what was it . . . da da da *da* da da da duh . . . 'Honky Tonk'! *Bad!* Bill Doggett. Remember? And the Coasters, the Dixie Hummingbirds, the Staple Singers—oooh!"

He would sing the words of the songs quietly to himself. He would hum the tunes. He would tap out the beats on his toy drums and try to play the melodies on his four-note harmonica. It frustrated him not to have real, grown-up instruments to play on, and it was hard for him to accept the fact that his mother just did not have enough money to buy real instruments for him. But luck soon proved to be with Stevie. Within the space of about a year and a half, he managed to acquire not one but *three* real instruments.

Every year the Detroit Lions Club gave a Christmas party for blind children, and at Christmastime during his first-grade year at school Stevie went to one. Each child received a gift, and someone must have told the Detroit Lions Club about Stevie's interest in music, for his gift—he could hardly believe it—was a set of real drums! Stevie sat down and began to pound on them right then and there.

Stevie was something of a favorite with the storekeepers and business people in the neighborhood. Often when his mother did her shopping she would take him with her, and he would listen to the sounds in the stores, and sniff the strange smells, and touch the objects in the displays. The shopkeepers, of course, remembered him because he was "the little blind boy," but they remembered him, too, because he almost always had something musical with him. At first it had been a little cardboard drum on a string around his neck, or his four-note toy harmonica. Later it was his radio, which accompanied him everywhere, even to the barbershop when his mother took him for a haircut. One time, the barber gave Stevie a harmonica—a real one. He practiced and practiced until he had mastered that.

Then, when he was seven, Stevie became the proud owner of a real piano. A neighbor was moving out of the housing project, and she really did not want to take her piano. Knowing how much Stevie loved music, she decided to give it to him. Stevie remembers, "I kept asking, 'When they gonna bring the piano over, Mamma?' I never realized how important that was going to be to me." When the piano finally arrived, it was like all the birthdays Stevie could remember all rolled into one. He ran his hands along the smooth wooden top, down the sides and around the back, down the slim legs, around to the cold metal of the pedals, and back up to the keys, some flat, some raised. He asked his mother to open the top of the piano, so he could feel the strings inside. He asked her what color they were. They were kind of gold, and the small wooden blocks between them were light brown. What color was the piano? A dark brown. From that moment on, dark brown, although he had not ever seen it and would never see it, meant something nice to Stevie. And since, he had been told, his skin was a sort of dark brown, too, he began to feel much better about his skin color.

Stevie got musical encouragement from another area as well. His mother was a member of Detroit's Whitestone Baptist Church, and she urged Stevie to join the junior choir. He had a very good voice, and before long he was singing lead parts in the choir's presentations. By the time he was nine or ten, he had been made a junior deacon in the church.

He loved church, for its services were filled with music. He especially liked it when the choir got to sing gospel songs, or when a guest singer was invited to the church to sing at special services. There seemed to be so much happiness in the church, and so much friendliness. There Stevie did not feel different; he felt that he really belonged. He made up his mind to be a minister when he grew up, which was not a completely farfetched goal for a little blind boy. There are a number of blind ministers in the United States.

Meanwhile Stevie continued to suffer from and to learn to cope with his blindness. "It wasn't until I was about eight or nine that I really started to get out and roam around by myself," Stevie recalls, "but I mostly had a sighted person with me so I was rarely put into situations where I was scared or would start to feel alone. I do remember one frightening thing, though. One time my father decided to take me out with him. I was pretty young—I must have been around seven or eight—he said to me, you want to go, Stevie, with me? We gonna go and get some candy and stuff, bubble gum and stuff . . . ride the bus and—c'mon! And I said okay, you know, and I was jumping up and down and was excited about it and we went over to this house and he had a piano over there and a saxophone—I never knew what one looked like— and I stayed there for a while, we stayed together . . . and then one day I remember him having to go off somewhere and he stayed away for a long time—and left me alone. That was the first time I got upset and I started to cry about that. But after a while I just said, hey, forget it, and I just went to sleep. I was just afraid because the surroundings weren't familar to me."

But in his own neighborhood the surroundings were familiar, the people were friends, and by the time he was nine or ten Stevie was a very popular member of the neighborhood. He was certainly the most gifted

musically, and he spent many Saturdays and after-
school hours on the front porches of neighbors' houses
on Horton Street. By this time Stevie had a set of
bongo drums, which he had mastered as he had every
other instrument to which he had been exposed.
Often he would play his bongos; sometimes it would
be the harmonica. Everyone would join in the singing,
but Stevie's clear, strong voice always took the lead.
Without exception the music was rhythm and blues,
the kind the people listened to on WCHB.

"I played Jimmy Reed's blues, Bobby Blue Bland's.
I used to sit by the radio and listen till sunup. Took a
little of everybody's style and made it my own."
He played like Ray Charles and tried copying his
singing style, to the delight of his listeners.

"We used to get pretty big crowds of people playing
on those porches," Stevie recalls. "I remember this one
time this lady who was a member of our church, she
was Sanctified Holiness, but she was still a member of
our church, the Whitestone Baptist Church, and she
came along and she said, 'Oh, Stevie, I'm ashamed
of you for playing that worldly music out here. I'm so
ashamed of you.' Ha, I really blew it, boy. I'd been a
junior deacon in the church and I used to sing solo at
the services. But she went and she told them what I
was doing and they told me to leave. And that's how I
became a sinner."

So much for Stevie's intention to become a
minister. He didn't think much of church any more,
especially of a church that could welcome a little boy

when he sang gospel songs and hymns and bar him for singing and playing rhythm and blues. He decided to be an engineer instead, or maybe a doctor. If his secret wish was to be an entertainer like Ray Charles, he did not share it with anyone.

Unable now to sing in church, Stevie spent even more time performing on neighbors' porches. One of his favorite singing partners was a boy about his age named John Glover. John Glover had a grown-up cousin named Ronnie White, who lived in another part of the city. Ronnie White was a member of the singing group The Miracles, which had enjoyed great success recording with a company named Hitsville USA. Of course, John Glover was very proud to have a cousin like Ronnie White, and he often boasted about him. John Glover was also proud to have a friend like Stevie. "You oughta hear my friend Stevie," he kept telling his cousin. But naturally White was busy, and he didn't really believe this kid Stevie was anything special. Then, one day in 1960, he happened to drop by to visit his relatives on Horton Street, and Stevie just happened to be having one of his front-porch sessions at the time. White did not have to listen very long to realize that his little cousin was right. This kid was something!

White arranged with the president of Hitsville USA, Berry Gordy, to take Stevie to the company's recording studio and to give him an audition, and one exciting afternoon Stevie was taken to the place that would be like a second home to him for the next ten years.

Stevie will never forget that afternoon. White took him around the studio, helping him to the different instruments and sound equipment, letting him touch them. It seemed to Stevie that every wonderful instrument in the world was right there in that sound studio, and he never wanted to leave it. Then he was introduced to Berry Gordy. Gordy listened to him sing, and play the harmonica and drums, and hired him on the spot, which says a lot for Gordy. Few, if any, other record-company owners would have taken such a chance back in 1960. But then, few if any other record companies had or would have the history of Gordy's. No other black-owned label would prevail as his would, and perhaps this was because once they were established, those other labels were too busy holding on to their position to take any risks or to try anything new.

Anyway, signing an artist brought in by a performer already with the company has become a common, and famous, practice of Gordy's. The Supremes were discovered by the Temptations. Diana Ross discovered the Jackson Five.

Of course, Stevie's mother actually signed Stevie's contract with Hitsville, for he was under age. There was little talk of money or other conditions. Stevie's family was so excited, so grateful for this opportunity for him, that they would have agreed to anything!

2
Motown

For Stevie, the recording studios at Hitsville USA, with all their wonderful instruments, were like a huge toy store to most kids. If he had been allowed to do so, he would have moved in permanently. As it was, he went there at three o'clock every day after school and stayed until dark. He went from instrument to instrument, playing them happily, mastering those he had not already learned to play well. Other artists would come to the studio for recording sessions, and Stevie would listen intently. Sometimes, because he was unable to see the red light which signaled that a record was being cut, he would burst in on a serious session. In fact, he was really something of a pest. But while his energy and interest were sometimes exasperating to the people at Hitsville, they had to admit he had talent, and they encouraged him to develop it.

At school, however, Stevie was not receiving the kind of encouragement from his teachers that might have been expected. Perhaps his teachers were afraid that he would not be able to deal with failure, and so were trying to keep him from getting his hopes up too high. Their lack of faith was understandable. After all, it wasn't exactly an everyday occurrence for a little blind black boy from the Detroit ghetto to make it in the music business. Fellow students were, out of jealousy, even more discouraging. "People at school told me I couldn't make it," Stevie recalls, "that I would end up making potholders instead. But after I thought I was going to be a musician, I became very determined simply to prove those people wrong."

During his first two years at Hitsville, Stevie learned the sound the company favored—a kind of slick, commercial rhythm and blues, mostly about love, mostly up-tempo, with a steady, identifiable beat, good to dance to. But even though he was very young, Stevie did not become a parrot. Stevie Wonder freely admits to borrowing from others in his early days, but he translated others' sounds into his own. If he had accepted the Hitsville musical formula completely, his first attempts at songwriting would have been typical of the company's songs. Instead, at the age of twelve, Stevie wrote two concertos! People around the studios started calling him the little boy wonder.

Stevie's first record was "You Made a Vow," which was released under the title, "Mother Thank You."

A forgettable, sentimental tune, it was an obvious attempt to exploit Stevie's young years. It did not sell well, but no one seemed to mind particularly. Certainly Stevie was so pleased simply to have made a record that was released that whether or not it was sold was a secondary consideration. His next recording, "I Call It Pretty Music," did better. But it wasn't memorable. It did not establish him as a star.

Then, at the age of twelve, Stevie recorded "Fingertips." Actually released in the early summer of 1963, it was one of those jumpy, crowd-swaying numbers, with a lot of screaming, and a kind of rising, crescendo-like quality that would excite the teen-age audience. It excited the Hitsville people, too, and it was decided that Stevie needed an exciting name to go with it. Clarence Paul, his conductor, called him Little Stevie. Others called him the little boy wonder. Someone came up with Little Stevie Wonder, and Gordy liked it. "I personally liked my real name better," says Stevie.

As expected, "Fingertips" was a smash hit, but no one could have foreseen that it would sell over a million copies and be No. 1 on the singles charts for fifteen weeks. After all, it was basically a novelty instrumental, featuring as it did an adolescent harmonica player and a live audience.

It consisted primarily of Stevie singing "Yeah, yeah, yeah," and Stevie playing a screeching harmonica. But Stevie had a way of singing "Yeah, yeah,

Stevie made his first trip abroad in 1963 when he was thirteen, following his first smash hit, "Fingertips." He appeared in a show in Paris Olympia Music Hall with British singer Louise Cordet. WIDE WORLD PHOTOS

yeah" that was different from the way anyone else had ever done it. He would later have the same success with "La, la, la, la, la, la," and "Do do wop" and a variety of other "riffs." And his harmonica playing was amazing. The screeches had purpose, and his range was remarkable. He had perfect control. But the secret of the tune's success was the sheer abandoned joy of this little twelve-year-old blind boy who had been given the chance to show what he could do and had done it. There could be no question in the mind of any listener that when he recorded that tune, Stevie Wonder was having the time of his life!

"Fingertips" was the biggest record Gordy had yet produced, and some in the music business have suggested that it *made* Berry Gordy. Certainly it helped him to establish his business more strongly.

In the music business, a hit single usually leads to the issuance of an album by the same artist. The single is on the album, and it helps sell the long-playing record. A few months later, Stevie's first album, "The Twelve-Year-Old Genius," was issued, although he was, of course, thirteen at the time. This did respectably well, primarily because it contained "Fingertips." At the age of thirteen, Stevie was a star.

This stardom had its good and bad sides. Like every other child star before and after him, Stevie found that his relationship with other kids in the neighborhood and at school just was not the same any more. The others were jealous. They decided that Stevie must be stuck-up, now that he was famous. He had to spend a great deal of time rehearsing and recording, but the other kids decided that his lack of time to play was because he was "too busy for his old friends." "The kids don't hardly speak to me," said Stevie wistfully at the age of thirteen. "I don't see them much. Sometimes I go to my friends' houses so they see I'm still the same."

He encountered difficulty as well at school, where he was mobbed every time he entered the school yard. Understandably, the school authorities disapproved of this disruption. "I remember," says Stevie, "when the people at the Board of Education said that I couldn't perform, that the Detroit schools couldn't accommodate my wanting to go on the road. I cried and cried and prayed for a long time."

Fortunately, in this case a solution was found. Stevie was taken out of the Detroit public schools and enrolled in the Michigan School for the Blind in Lansing, some one hundred fifty miles from Detroit. There the curriculum was more flexible, and with the understanding that he would be accompanied by a private tutor provided by Hitsville and would study several hours each day while on the road, Stevie was able to tour with the group of Hitsville performers who traveled around doing mostly one-night stands.

It is hard to know how much the songs themselves and Stevie's voice contributed to the success of his records, and how much this success was due to the fact that he was thirteen years old and blind. Sighted people have a great deal of sympathy for the blind—perhaps pity is a better word. In Stevie's case, the sentiment of many was: "Oh look at that poor little blind boy. Isn't it nice that he is musically talented. Otherwise, what can he expect out of life?" Also, Stevie was young, and people think that very young stars are cute. A little blind musical talent is particularly cute, and something of a curiosity.

41

Like other blind performers, big and little, Stevie exhibited what are called "blindisms." These are rhythmic movements of the body and the head such as rubbing the eyes, swaying and rocking, etc.

Stevie explains, "When you're blind you build up a lot of excess energy that other people get rid of through their eyes. You got to work it off some way, you know, and it's just an unconscious thing. Like, a lot of blind people are always rubbing their eyes. Each person develops his own blindism."

Stevie's most common blindism was to throw his head back and move it from side to side. He did this especially when he was happy, and when he was making music he was always happy. Thus, when he performed live or on television, he was remembered more clearly by audiences than a sighted performer would be—even a twelve- or thirteen-year-old sighted performer.

But Stevie's performances were memorable for other reasons, the chief reason being that he was a natural-born entertainer. When he was younger, he had entertained his family with his ability to mimic other people's voices. Later he had entertained his neighbors by playing and singing on their front porches. It was only natural, then, that he would enjoy performing in front of an entire auditorium or hall. Few artists can get an audience going with him as well as Stevie Wonder can, and this was nearly as true of Little Stevie Wonder as it is of Stevie Wonder the young man. He loved his audiences. "When *I* look out at an audience," he explains, "all I see are beautiful people." Naturally he was grateful to them for supporting him, enabling him to do what he loved best.

But his relationship with an audience went deeper than that. Because he was blind, he lived in a very private, inner world, and that world got pretty lonely sometimes. It was also so self-contained that it produced great pressure on a very young boy. Performing before an audience provided a kind of emotional release, an escape from himself. Often he ignored the fact that his number was over and it was time to make his exit, and would pay no attention to the frantic whispers from backstage pleading with him to say good-by to the audience. Sometimes he had to be removed bodily from the stage. "I used to pick him up and carry him him off," Clarence Paul remembers.

Stevie was on the road nearly every weekend, and perhaps two additional weeks each month. In between performing and studying he played his instruments, wrote songs, and recorded new records. His second album, "Jazz Soul of Little Stevie," was released when he was thirteen, and he practiced signing his name for days before, knowing that the employees at Hitsville USA would want autographed copies. After autographing an album cover for Berry Gordy, Stevie joked, "This is the very best signature that I have ever seen."

To many, Stevie's life must have seemed enviable.

A star at such a young age, all that money, all those clothes! On tour, everywhere he went, crowds mobbed him, trying to touch him, thrusting autograph books into his face. Now, when he listened to the radio he heard his own songs. But glamorous though it may have seemed, Stevie's was a very lonely life; in many ways even lonelier than it had been before he signed with Hitsville. He had no friends his age. While he knew kids his age at Michigan School for the Blind, he was so often away on tour that there was no opportunity to develop strong friendships. His fellow performers, with whom he traveled, were all considerably older than he, for he was Hitsville's only child star. He spent most of his time with adults—his tutor, Ted Hall, his music teacher, Mrs. Adena Johnston, and his arranger, Clarence Paul, who also acted as a stand-in father, brother, and friend.

He saw his family only rarely. Michigan School for the Blind was too far away from Detroit for him to commute, and when he was not at school he was on tour. Above all he missed his mother, and long telephone calls had to take the place of in-person talks. Stevie came to love that instrument equally as much as his musical instruments.

Hitsville USA became his family and was, in many ways, more strict than his real family would have been. Under the close watch of his tutor, Ted Hall, Stevie did indeed study several hours a day, and the B average he maintained at school was proof of his hard work. Hall taught him more than schoolbook subjects. He also taught him the "right values," such as hard work and honesty. Swearing was not allowed, nor was smoking. Stevie, whose records were selling millions of dollars' worth, had an allowance of exactly $2.50 a week, and that was it. "Sometimes he spends it all," said Mrs. Johnston when Stevie was thirteen, "and then he whispers in my ear, 'I'm broke.' I whisper back, 'I'm broke, too.' We hope to teach him to use his money wisely, to avoid champagne tastes."

That went for the rest of the family, too. Stevie's mother was allowed enough of Stevie's earnings to cover expenses at home, but she had no actual control of the money her son made. After Stevie had signed with Hitsville, the company had a court-appointed attorney named as his legal guardian who saw to it that most of Stevie's earnings went into a trust fund. He would not be able to get at the money until he was twenty-one years old.

Stevie wanted to buy a house for his mother, but he could not. He had to be content with little gifts which he bought with his allowance, and he bought something for her on every trip. He wanted to buy musical instruments to play when he was at home, but this was not allowed either. Instead, Gordy gave him a tape recorder.

Mealtimes and bedtime were on a regular schedule. In fact, with scheduled concerts, scheduled study hours, scheduled music lessons, Stevie's life was structured almost to the point of stiflement. But if Stevie ever resented it, he did not show it. "I was just another little blind boy before I came to Hitsville. That was the best thing that ever happened to me," he said fervently when he was thirteen. "No, I really mean that."

There were ways in which this life was ideal for Stevie—more so since he was blind than if he had been sighted. Adolescence and early teen age are difficult stages for everyone. At no time in life are one's emotional ups and downs more extreme. It is the time of the deepest identity crisis and the most severe feelings of self-consciousness. And if it is hard for the non-handicapped teen-ager to get through these years, it is usually doubly hard for the handicapped teen-ager. Non-handicapped teen-agers are self-conscious about their physical appearance. They worry that their ears are too big or their noses are too long. When they go out in public, they are sure that everyone is looking at them and noticing any defects, real or imagined. Imagine how self-conscious a handicapped teen-ager feels.

More than anything else, a teen-ager wants to be part of a group, like others his age. If his friends wear certain clothes, can stay out late at night, drive cars, that's what he wants to do. Many handicapped teen-agers are prevented from participating in usual teen-age activities such as dancing or driving cars or riding motorcycles.

The teen-age years are also a time of looking to the future, to marriage and a family of their own in some cases, to a career in others. The handicapped teen-ager cannot look forward to the same things with any degree of confidence. Many have no assurance that they will find anyone to love them, and, worse, most cannot look forward with any confidence to a career that matches their capabilities. It is very hard to face a life of dependence on others.

The life Stevie led as a teen-ager protected him from many of these teen-age crises. First, in the world in which he moved he had little reason for feeling self-conscious about his appearance. Many handicapped teen-agers dread the discovery by other people of their handicaps. In Stevie's world, nearly everyone with whom he came in contact already knew he was blind. He rarely found himself in situations where he was forced to ask a stranger for help. He was surrounded by people whose job was to help him.

Had Stevie lived at home and gone to school regularly like other teen-agers, he would have felt his differentness more strongly. He would have heard the bigger boys talk about motorcycles and cars and the younger boys talk about getting their driver's licenses, and he would have felt left out. But Stevie rarely spent much time around non-handicapped teen-agers.

Though blind and black, at sixteen Stevie Wonder was one of the luckiest teen-agers in the world. Unlike others his age, he knew what he was going to do; and what's more, he was already doing it. UNITED PRESS INTERNATIONAL PHOTO

At school the kids shared his handicap; out of school he spent his time with adults.

As for his future, Stevie did not share the wonder and worry of other teen-agers. He knew what he was going to do; he was already doing it!

Certainly Stevie had his share of adolescent identity crises, his share of depression and frustration over his blindness. But he was remarkably well adjusted, considering his age and his handicap. Naturally reporters were always asking him questions related to his blindness. Once, when he was thirteen, he was asked if he could see for one minute what he would most like to see. He answered solemnly, "If I could see for one minute, man, I could see the whole world. Whatever I saw that one minute would be the whole world."

By the time Stevie was fourteen, Berry Gordy had changed the name of his company to Motown, a contraction of Motor Town, which black inhabitants of Detroit called the city where so many automobiles are made. Thanks in no small measure to Stevie, Gordy's company was making good money, and soon after the creation of the label, Motown would have its first big hit. Smokey Robinson and the Miracles, the group to which Stevie's discoverer, Ronnie White, belonged, did "Shop Around." The song became a minor rhythm and blues classic. Other performers added to that success. The Four Tops, who are perhaps best known for "Reach Out (I'll Be There)," had signed with Gordy in 1962. Motown could also boast Marvin Gaye, Mary Wells, and the Temptations, and in 1964, when Stevie was fourteen, a group of three teen-age girls came to Motown, none other than The Supremes.

All in all, it was quite a roster of talents, but they would have to wait some years before they received their true share of success. They were in large measure unknown to the mass white audience. It was the 1960s, and for the white audience in those years music primarily meant the Beatles. While much of the Beatles' material represented a direct borrowing from black sources, the majority of the audience did not realize it. It was white rock groups that got on the "Ed Sullivan Show" and had access to other forums of mass exposure. No Motown performers got on those shows.

Yet, to look at or watch the Motown performers, no one would have known that they were not internationally famous. They were highly polished and professional acts, every one of them.

Gordy realized that good live performances sell records, and even when he did not really have the money to spend, he spent it on choreography and costuming. In those early days his artists were playing primarily to audiences of young ghetto kids, but they were dressed as if to play at Las Vegas. This fact was not lost on their young audiences. When those performers danced, they didn't just jump all over the stage, as some performers did. Their movements, even in slow numbers, were perfectly coordinated. And every show they did, every number they did, they did as if they were performing at the White House. They were talented all right, but their talent was presented in a quality package. An audience at a performance of Motown stars got its money's worth and then some, and when the shows were over the kids went out and bought Motown records.

Little Stevie Wonder was coached and chore-ographed equally as much as the older performers, although certain allowances were made for his youthfulness. If Marvin Gaye had had to be carried bodily offstage, he would have been fired! Stevie was dressed in glitter-trimmed suits—and probably more was spent on his clothes than on those of some other male performers, because he was growing a lot faster than they were. His harmonica was polished to a gleaming shine, and his name was emblazoned in glitter on his drums. He needed no coaching in enthusiasm—in fact, he had to be constantly reminded that there would be other performances; he needn't give his whole life to this evening's. Polish. Perfection. Cool. Over and over the Motown performers were schooled in these qualities, and the fact that Stevie Wonder became a polished professional is due in no small measure to Berry Gordy's formula.

There was one particular aspect of Stevie's behavior that, try as they might, the Motown people could not change – his tendency to lateness. He simply had never developed the same concept of time that most people have. Most people who understand blindness regard Stevie's lateness as characteristic of his condition. Since he cannot see the light of day or the darkness of night, he does not divide his days and nights the way others do. This may be the reason. It may also be, however, that by being late all the time, Stevie was engaging in one small rebellion against the sighted world. He had to depend so much on sighted people, had constantly to seek their assistance. In a sense, his lateness was a way of asserting his independence from the sighted world in general and Motown in particular.

Meanwhile Stevie's fame continued to rest basically upon "Fingertips." His second album, "Jazz Soul of Little Stevie," had not done particularly well, and his singles were hardly smash hits. Four months after the release of "Fingertips," "Work Out, Stevie, Work Out" was released; it only reached No. 33 on the singles charts. His two 1964 singles, "Castles in the Sand" and "Hey, Harmonica Man," reached Nos. 52 and 29, respectively.

In the fall of 1965 came a vocal version of "High Heel Sneakers," but it went nowhere, and there was some question that Stevie would ever cut a record that would do as well as "Fingertips." But then, that winter, his recording of "Uptight (Everything's All Right)" was released. It reached No. 3 on the singles charts, and it showed that there was more to Stevie

Wonder than his other records had indicated. Primarily, it revealed that he had a truly exciting voice. As one writer put it, the wild innocence of his harmonica playing carried over into his singing. Partly, this quality of his voice was due to his youth; he was only fifteen and was unlikely to have a disciplined voice at that age. Partly, too, it was due to his blindness: he had learned to express in his voice the emotions that he could not express in his eyes or on his face in the same way as sighted people could. In many ways he played his voice like a musical instrument, and so, while the words of his songs were emotional ones, sung in his voice they went beyond emotionalism.

Still his songs were pretty much of the typical Motown formula. Motown songs were almost all very bubbly, very romantic, and very popular, for they expressed the romantic feelings of every normal teenager; Berry Gordy and the other heads of the company were quite rigid in sticking to that formula. Stevie caught on to the formula early, and beginning with "Uptight," released when he was sixteen, he collaborated with the Motown writers and lyricists on most of the material he recorded, and his name was included in the credits.

Meanwhile, however, Stevie's own musical horizons were being expanded. No rock 'n' roll or rhythm and blues was played under the tutelage of his blind music teacher at the Michigan School for the Blind.

There he was taught to play and to understand Bach and Chopin, and Stevie got his knuckles "whumped" if he strayed from the classical forms. While at thirteen he insisted, "I am going to stick to my own style 'cause everybody likes it better including me," in later years he would be grateful for that formal musical training, which would help him move out of the Motown mold.

Stevie insists that he was never as deep into the Motown mold as other artists or songwriters with the label were, though. "I never felt that I strictly embodied the Motown sound," he says. "I mean there weren't too many people around there doing white-folk stuff like 'Blowin' in the Wind,' or 'Mr. Tambourine Man,' like I was."

Stevie was fifteen years old when he decided he should record "Blowin' in the Wind," and when he first suggested the idea he met with strong resistance at Motown. Motown was primarily a dance-record label, and even when it did go in for ballads, they certainly weren't white, Peter, Paul and Mary-type folk songs. But Stevie insisted; the song expressed things he was feeling, and he wanted to record it. Motown finally gave in, and the record was fairly successful, reaching No. 9 on the singles charts and staying there for ten weeks, although critics called it "soupy." So, for that matter, was "A Place in the Sun," his next record to be released. In both, his voice was quite disciplined, and neither song was quite the vehicle for his "letting it all hang out," with respect to his voice. But if anyone had decided his voice had lost its "wild innocence," "I Was Made to Love Her," released in 1967, proved this wrong.

Stevie's mother helped him write the song. "I wrote the melody and chord structure," Stevie recalls, "but she came up with the phrases. It was the first time she worked on a song with me. It really delighted her. She used to be a gospel singer."

The song ranked No. 2 on the singles charts for fifteen weeks. It was given critical praise as well, although it was not so much the song that excited the attention of music critics: the range of his voice, which, once again, he played like a musical instrument, was remarkable.

During his late teens Stevie included in his albums quite a few songs that had been done by other artists, among them "Water Boy," "Alfie," and "Traveling Man." When he expressed his desire to do such songs he met with some resistance, as he had when he wanted to record "Blowin' in the Wind." But he insisted, and prevailed most of the time. These songs expressed what he wanted to say, and he saw no reason not to make his feelings known through the songs of others, songs not of the Motown mold.

Stevie was a highly sensitive young boy, and if the words of a song touched him he wanted to do that song, no matter with what race or musical style it was associated. And when he sang a song like "Blowin' in the Wind," it was as if no one had ever sung it before.

Rochelle Larkin, a friend of this author's who has written a book on soul music, remembers going to a concert in which Stevie sang "Blowin' in the Wind": "He sang it at a concert that was a complete bomb, except for him," she says. "Outdoors, in an enormous baseball field, horrible acoustics, cold and rainy. By the end of the first half, everyone, including the promoters, had wished they'd stayed home. Towards the end of the second half, Stevie Wonder came out and sang "Blowin' in the Wind" as if that song had never been sung before. Suddenly he wasn't 'Little' Stevie Wonder any more. He came out of the child-entertainer, novelty category and brought the crowd to its feet. He had reached for something and had caught it, and there was no longer a boy Wonder, but a man."

Once he began to record songs that had been written or recorded by others, some observers began to forecast the demise of Stevie Wonder. He just did not seem to "have it" anymore, some theorized. Many who had called him a genius when he was sixteen pronounced him washed up at seventeen. While it is true that his three recordings after "I Was Made to Love Her" only made numbers 9, 12, and 35 on the charts, it was a bit early to pronounce Stevie a washout. But some insisted that he had gone as far as he could go, had grown as a singer and musician as much as he could grow.

Growth, as a matter of fact, had much to do with this period of Stevie's career. Stevie was indeed growing—physically, mentally, and emotionally. He was going through changes in all these areas, and his music was affected by all three. Physically, he was now Little Stevie Wonder in name only. While he was still slim, he was nearly six feet tall, and he was shaving. He did not any longer fit the image of boy genius, and yet he was not quite a man. Then, too, his voice had changed, which was natural for a teen-aged boy but a potentially difficult problem for a young singer. He had to get used to this new voice, to find its range and understand its possibilities. It was a challenge for Stevie, and though it took some time, eventually he adjusted to his new voice.

Even more seriously affecting his career were his mental and emotional changes. While he was almost totally immersed in music, he was keenly aware of the outside world and of the manner in which that world viewed a young man like him. Older now, and more self-assured, he can joke about it, assuming a high, falsetto voice: "Oooh, you not only born black, boy. You born black and blind!" But it really is not now, and it certainly was not then, a joking matter.

Personally, Stevie had been shielded in some ways from the impact of racial discrimination. It could have been more difficult for him if he had not worked for a black owned and managed company. And yet there were times when he felt his tutors and mentors would not have been as strict with him if he had not been black. They had shown the kind of defensive puritanism that held that big spending, too much flashiness, even improper language were part of the white-held stereotype of blacks and that blacks should avoid all such behavior in order to be acceptable.

But no young black person, no matter how protected, can escape the devastating effects of prejudice or be unaware of the racial climate in the larger society. Stevie Wonder went through his teens during the 1960s, and in those years, his most impressionable, America experienced the greatest period of racial unrest in its history. When Stevie was fifteen Watts, the poor black section of Los Angeles, erupted in riots. A month before Stevie turned eighteen Martin Luther King, Jr., was assassinated, and Stevie's own community of Detroit was the scene of massive looting and burning. Riots in other cities followed. Though he could not see them on television, he could feel the charged atmosphere. And he could hear the anti-white and anti-black statements that flew back and forth between the two sides. The atmosphere of hatred disturbed Stevie, who was basically a peace-loving young man. It was hard for him to understand a society in which race could make so much difference. Years later he wrote in a song:

Why must my color black make me a lesser man?
I thought this world was made for every man.

It was still hard, too, for him to adjust to his blindness. No handicap is ever accepted. Instead, it is adjusted to, and that kind of adjustment is often a lifelong process. He was seventeen now, and like any other person his age, he yearned for independence. But independence is not fully possible for a blind person. He could not just go out by himself; always someone would have to accompany him. Like any other young man, he was interested in girls, but though girls screamed at his performances, mobbed him on the street, begged for his autograph, he did not have any real dates. He refused to go on a date with a chaperone, and he was embarrassed to ask a date to help him in and out of cars or to tell him what was happening in a movie. Besides, his life was so closely supervised by the people at Motown that he had little opportunity to meet girls even if he wanted to.

By age seventeen, Stevie was also beginning to feel too tightly bound by the strict rules under which his life was governed by Motown. Naturally his allowance was now considerably larger than $2.50 per week, but Stevie felt he was entitled to more. He also felt that no one around Motown realized he was no longer Little Stevie. He was a man now, and he wanted to be treated like one.

Finally, he felt confined by the Motown formula. Despite the fact that he made solid hits out of "Shoo-be-oo-be-oo-be-oo-da-day," "My Cherie Amour," and "Signed, Sealed and Delivered," all of which he wrote, he was no longer comfortable with the slick and glossy Motown sound that had commercial soul, but no soul in the true sense of the word. He had things to say that just did not fit into the mold.

In short, Stevie went through an extremely difficult time for three or four years. Added to his emotional and physical changes were the changes that were occurring in the music world. Traditional rock was going out; acid rock was coming in. His own musical identity was in transition, and lack of hit records caused worry and heightened emotional strain. What if he was washed up? What if his career was ending? What in the world would he, a blind person, do if he could not make it in music when music was all he knew?

Desperate, Stevie considered drugs. He knew many musicians who used them, many people who insisted they were more sensitive and creative when they were on drugs than at other times. Perhaps drugs would help him too. Just a few uppers to give him more energy when he was depressed. Just a few downers to help him think more clearly when his mind was over-active. Had he been on his own, Stevie could have gotten into serious trouble.

Fortunately, however, the people at Motown recognized his restlessness and worry and realized what it could lead to. It took a high degree of watch-fulness, and hours of talking spread over months, to convince him that if he turned to drugs he would really be washed up. At long last, Stevie understood that they were right. "If I were high it would destroy the character of my music," he says, "because I would be tripping out so much on myself as opposed to the things around me, or what I was seeing as opposed to the conclusions I've come to within my mind."

Like other musicians, Stevie is often thought to be on drugs. Drug taking is widely regarded as an "occupational hazard" in the music world. Stevie is one musician who does not take drugs.

"I never did acid or anything like that," he says, "but I did try grass a couple of times. The first time was pretty nice, I got out there, but the next time was nothing but a lot of paranoia so I never went near it again. I love to hear people talking about all the junk I must be doing, though. You know, 'There goes Stevie Wonder jivin' around. Must be stoned again.' Sometimes I'll be sitting somewhere listening to tapes, like on a plane or something, and my head'll get to going around like it does when I hear music, and I'll hear somebody whisper, 'Look at Stevie Wonder over there actin' crazy. You reckon he on dope?' That's so funny. First of all, they figure that 'cause you're blind you can't hear them. And my moving my head around like that, that's just what is called a blindism."

By later teen age, Stevie had conquered his other blindisms, and when he was not making or listening to music he did not move his head back and forth in that lolling motion except when he was laughing or

61

very happy. But when he was making or listening to music, he simply could not control that outlet for his energy. This led to another source of disappointment for Stevie. American television producers were hesitant to use him, for they felt it would make the audience nervous to watch him move his head around. During those years, more than ever, he needed that kind of exposure, and it was denied him in the United States.

The management of supper clubs did not share this hesitancy, and in addition to continuing to tour with other Motown stars and doing personal live concerts, Stevie began to appear at such clubs as the Cellar Door in Washington, D.C., and the Village Gate in New York City. Despite the lack of hit singles, his popularity continued.

Then, in late 1968 "For Once in My Life" was released and became a solid hit, reaching No. 2 on the charts. "I Don't Know Why," released early in 1969, did not do very well, but "My Cherie Amour," released in May of the same year, reached the No. 4 position; and "Yester Me, Yester You, Yesterday," released in October, 1969, reached the No. 7 position. His single "Signed, Sealed, Delivered, I'm Yours," released in June the following year, made No. 3. Also in 1970 he appeared at one of the premier entertainment showcases, the Copacabana in New York City. His appearance there received rave reviews. Anyone who was called "an honest prodigy of flawless taste and superb talent," was definitely not washed up.

In the same year the first album Stevie produced himself, "Signed, Sealed and Delivered," was released. It was a remarkable achievement for one so young. But Stevie had enjoyed the unique experience of having the run, in effect, of a fully equipped recording studio. While at first Stevie had been most concerned with playing every instrument in the place, over the years he had become interested in and familiar with nearly every aspect of the recording and producing process. "Signed, Sealed and Delivered" won an award for best soul album of 1970.

By that time, although it had taken a couple of years, Stevie had resolved most of the problems that had disturbed him. One major helpful influence was that of Syreeta Wright, a former secretary at Motown whose true ambition was to be a singer-songwriter. After they had gotten to know each other, she and Stevie spent hours talking about their shared interest in music, and after a time they fell in love. They were married in 1970.

One problem Stevie had not resolved was his relationship with Motown. He still yearned to break away from the company's formula, to establish the independence of his musical thinking. This desire is evident in the second album he produced, in 1970 when he was twenty. It was titled "Where I'm Coming From," and quite literally it showed that Stevie Wonder had matured greatly and that while his music was still greatly influenced by Motown, he was

Stevie and Syreeta Wright announced their engagement in London on June 30, 1970. As both were deeply committed to careers in music, they looked forward to a life of musical collaboration. UNITED PRESS INTERNATIONAL PHOTO

developing a style that would be his own—not Ray Charles', not Motown's, not anyone else's. Written entirely by Stevie and Syreeta, the songs are uneven in quality. Lyrically they are unremarkable, and seem to be reaching too far for uniqueness, contemporariness. But the music is radically different from Stevie's

64

earlier work. He played drums, piano, and harmonica in ways that his fans had never heard before. And his voice, played like a musical instrument, exploited its own qualities for new kinds of meaning.

Clearly, Stevie Wonder had come a long way in the decade since his signing by Motown.

3
His Own Man

Stevie turned twenty-one on May 13, 1971, and that birthday signaled a number of major changes in his life, some under his control, some not. Perhaps the most important event that occurred as a result of his reaching twenty-one was that his trust fund, established by his court-appointed guardian when he was signed by Berry Gordy, was now available to him. Even though expense money for Stevie and his family had been taken out consistently over the years, it contained over one million dollars. There have been other twenty-one-year-old millionaires in history, even self-made twenty-one-year-old millionaires, but the number is not high. For Stevie, the money meant many things, but most of all it meant that he could pursue his dreams. He could afford to hire a recording studio and produce his own records, and that is exactly what he decided to do.

First, he called in an outside auditor to check that he had been treated fairly by Motown. This was not an unheard-of thing to do. Many entertainers under contract to a company or studio do the same. What makes the audit of Motown's books by Stevie's outside auditor noteworthy is that Motown was, and still is, highly secretive about its finances. For a single to become a gold record it must sell a million copies; an LP must sell half a million copies to be a gold album. Naturally, it is the record companies themselves who keep these figures, and they must be verified by someone outside the company. Motown is the only major record company that refuses to submit to a public audit in order to have its gold records certified by the Recording Industry Association of America. Thus, its operations and finances have often been suspect. But if there are any grounds for suspicion of Motown's financial operations, they cannot be found in their handling of Stevie Wonder's account. His auditor verified Motown's figures.

That matter settled, Stevie asked for his contract back from Motown. Ewert Abner, president of Motown, recalls, "He came to me and said, 'I'm twenty-one now. I'm not gonna do what you say anymore. Void my contract.' I freaked."

"They were upset at first," Stevie says now. He does not like to talk about the bad feelings that his decision created at the company. He feels there is no point in bringing up old unpleasantness. "But," he continues, "they began to understand—later. Whatever peak I had reached doing that kind of music, I had reached. It was important for them to understand we were going nowhere.

"I wasn't growing," he explains; "I just kept repeating the Stevie Wonder sound, and it didn't express how I felt about what was happening out there. I decided to go for something besides a winning formula. I wanted to see what would happen if I changed. It challenged me to give the public something other than what it was used to hearing."

He wanted to strike out on his own, and no amount of arguing could persuade him to change his mind. Naturally people at Motown accused him of being ungrateful and warned him that he would be much better off remaining with an established label, benefiting from the technology of its recording studios and its massive publicity and distribution apparatus, than trying to make a go of it on an independent basis.

Some people who had no personal stake in the matter agreed with Motown. Stevie's intended move would cost a lot of money, even for a millionaire; he would lose all the benefits he had enjoyed with Motown and would take on a bushel of headaches. He would need to form his own companies, make distribution contacts, be responsible for his own bookings. The music business, like most other businesses, is high-powered. Talent is not enough: one needs a high degree of knowledge and cleverness, or at least must be smart enough to pick advisers with those qualities. Like most of the other Motown stars, Stevie was unschooled in finance, and no lawyer had ever helped him negotiate a contract. Being blind, Stevie had been forced to rely on others for many things. How could he avoid being exploited and poorly advised on the ins and outs of the business?

But Stevie would not be talked out of it. Shortly after he turned twenty-one, he left Motown. With a quarter of the million dollars that had been held in trust for him, he rented a recording studio in New York and began the journey to himself that he had yearned to embark on for several years. "I was twenty-one," Stevie recalls; "I had no company but decided to invest all my money in the kind of music that I had never been able to get into before. I barricaded myself into the studios with all the instruments I could think of. . . ."

Stevie and Syreeta set to work writing songs to be produced by Stevie's own company, Taurus Productions, and published by his own publishing company, Black Bull, Inc.

Needless to say, Stevie Wonder is into astrology. As he was born on May 13, his sun sign is Taurus, the bull. He does not feel that his belief in astrology conflicts with his belief in God, and he has never questioned the existence of God. Perhaps it is easier for one who is blind to believe in things that cannot be seen.

Of course, Stevie did not break away from Motown

and establish his own production and publishing companies all alone. He needed lawyers, advisers, a road manager, numerous other staff people; but Stevie seems to have done a very good job choosing them. He chose people not merely to run his affairs for him but also to keep him informed of their activities, in order that he might learn from them. Just as he had not been content merely to write and perform music but had learned how to produce records as well, so he would learn the legal and financial aspects of recording.

One of his most fortunate choices was Ira Tucker for his publicist. Tucker was the brother of Linda Lawrence, who had been one of the Supremes and who had for a while sung with the Wonder band. Stevie and Tucker became good friends. It was a little hard for Tucker to adjust to the life style that Stevie had in mind—no regular hours, constant movement, music everywhere, people everywhere. But while his is sometimes a very difficult job, he believes it is worth all the hassles to be associated with someone whom he considers a true genius. "And he's out there, Jack, I mean it," Tucker will say. "He exists on a whole other plane than the rest of us."

Stevie also had "family" on whom to rely. His brother, Calvin, became an important part of his organization.

Meanwhile Stevie was learning more about music, or more specifically, more about how to make music.

He was learning about the Arp and Moog synthesizers. "A synthesizer," Stevie explains, "has to be programmed. It consists of seven or eight oscillators and the sound has to be created, because it's just another electrical impulse. With it, you have the ability to shape the melody into any form you desire: attack, sustain, delay, release or the combination of those can be done any way you want to create the sound. You can only play one note at a time, though, with the synthesizer, so I use the Moog for certain horn lines, but it really is not so much to imitate as to make the horizon for an instrument even wider.

"I also use the Arp synthesizer, which I program myself and have become very attached to."

With the help of the synthesizers, Stevie was able to do all the parts of a number himself, to control every aspect of the sound, the balance, the total effect. He was able to play most of the instrumental accompaniments—piano, drums, harmonica, organ, clavichord—and to sing most of his own background vocals. It was a time in his life comparable only to that some ten years before when, having signed with Motown, he had access to the wonderful world of its recording studios. Stevie spent hours on end experimenting with the synthesizers, orchestrating numbers, and getting down on tape the ideas he had stored up for years. With release from the pressures he had felt with Motown, new ideas came like torrents, and in his rush to set them down he often forgot to eat or sleep. It was the beginning of a period of tremendous productivity for Stevie.

He now had the chance he longed for, to produce a record album in its entirety, and though producing an album is a tremendously complex and costly enterprise, Stevie loved every minute of it. The forty-plus separate tracks on which instruments can be recorded excited rather than daunted him. Album production often involves spending fifty hours straight in the recording studios. Concentrating intently for so long without sleep, the body eventually begins to function as if on automatic pilot, although the mind remains alert. Stevie thrived on that kind of schedule.

"Music of My Mind," was a remarkable departure from his previous work. In it there was much less of the sweetness and airiness that had characterized his songs, and the instrumentation was no longer in the traditional Motown vein, designed to achieve sweet emotional effect. Not only was there now definite musical progress, but the words of the songs were more timely, more meaningful, more aware. It was his first "concept" album. The synthesizers enabled him to give a more mental flavor to his compositions and a rock flavor that had never been present before. His work was still high in emotional content, but with his new instrumental freedom and with the help of the synthesizer, it became more profound. Referring to the synthesizers, Stevie has said, "They express what's inside my mind."

The album proved that the gamble Stevie had taken was worth it. "That's when I really broke out," he says now. Stevie had proved what he had known all along. "Record companies . . . ," he says, "who naturally assume that they know everything there is to know . . . they're telling you what you can and cannot do. What the public will *accept*. But like, how do they know they won't accept something if nobody ever does it?"

"One-man recordings have been tried by other performers," said one critic, ". . . but no one had brought off the complicated trick of playing most or all of the parts better than Wonder in this collection. . . . After a few minutes of the first track, one promptly forgets all about the technical [considerations] and settles down to hear a constantly provocative flow of musical ideas, good humor, artistic invention and solid swing."

"Music of My Mind" was truly the work of a new, more mature, more independent Stevie Wonder, and if Stevie were ever to change his name, then would have been the time to do it. He could have shed the name Motown had given him just as he had shed the other Motown strictures. "But I've had the name Wonder for so long now that people connect it up with their concept of me," says Stevie. While he did consider changing his name, perhaps going back to his real name, he did not actually do it. Stevie Wonder he would remain.

Stevie was prepared to advertise and distribute the album himself. Although he could hardly do so as well as Motown could, he valued his independence too highly to return to the company for help. Fortunately he didn't have to. Instead Motown came to him, with an offer to renew his contract under terms unheard of for Motown and practically unheard of in the record business as a whole. Instead of receiving all the writing royalties as the company usually did, Motown would split the royalties half and half with Stevie. He would have the right to record when, where, and how he wanted to and also to decide which cuts would be released as singles. His own Taurus Productions, Inc., would produce his work, and his own Black Bull Music, Inc., would publish it. Says Stevie, "All Motown does for us now is distribute the records and give them some push." Thus Stevie Wonder and Motown were reunited, but on a basis that was much different from the old. Stevie would have a strong financial position, and almost complete artistic freedom. While once the entertainer and the company had maintained almost a father-son relationship, now they had a true partnership.

Even though under the agreement it was Motown who was responsible for publicity and distribution of Stevie's records, in the summer of 1972 Stevie decided to take some of that responsibility upon himself as well. The Rolling Stones were scheduled to tour the

United States that summer, and Stevie was offered the opportunity to tour with them as the opening act of their show. Realizing that by accepting the offer he could publicize his album better than in any other way, and eager for the opportunity for so many live performances, Stevie agreed, and it proved to be one of the key moves of his career.

While it was hard to be cast in the role of warming up audiences for the Stones, Stevie said during the tour, "The tour has been good for me. At least it lets people know I'm not doing 'Fingertips' anymore." The idea was exposure.

While most black music lovers had followed Stevie since "Fingertips," many whites knew comparatively little about him. They remembered "Fingertips," of course, and his other hit singles like "Yester Me, Yester You, Yesterday" and "My Cherie Amour." But they were not aware of the lesser-known cuts on his albums, or of his new material. The Rolling Stones tour gave this largely untouched audience a chance to hear the new Stevie Wonder, and they were highly impressed. By the time the tour ended, with Stevie joining Mick Jagger in a memorable rendition of "Satisfaction," Stevie's audience had tripled and his renown as a major musician had expanded from the smaller world of the old-line Stevie Wonder fans and the music critics to the larger world of the mass national audience.

The timing was perfect, for it was just about at that time that white rock music was declining and the public was ripe for the sounds of black popular music. White rock music seemed to have lost its creative energy, and instead of coming up with exciting sounds, white rock entertainers opted instead for exciting looks—transvestite glitter, self-conscious weirdness, and exhibitionism. Mick Jagger started to wear eye shadow, Elton John adopted his famous space garb, and Alice Cooper started wearing boa constrictors. They, and the mood they established, represented the height of alienation. While audiences came away from their concerts having been bombarded with visual excitement, the music did not stay with them. It had little meaning. Then along came Stevie Wonder to introduce them to black music, which did have meaning, which relied on its melodies and lyrics to touch the heart and soul. The mass audience certainly did not shut out white rock music; what it did was to welcome black music, too, to complete what was lacking in the other. As one critic put it, ". . . now it's black people who seem to have some notion of how to survive the bleak-looking years to come, how to feel both happy and responsible, how to love my brother without being taken by him and, above all, how to endure."

In November of 1972, "Superstition" was released, and it proved to be the record that really put Stevie

*Stevie joins Mick Jagger in a rousing rendition of "Satisfaction"
to close the show during his 1972 tour with the Rolling
Stones. The tour gained Stevie exposure and tripled his
audience.* WARTOKE CONCERN, INC.

out in front again. It was sound lyrically, but its popularity is due primarily to its music. In recording it, Stevie had wired the Arp synthesizer to the clavinet, or electric piano, to produce an incessant and distinctive wop-wop sound that was unforgettable. "Superstition" hit No. 1 on the singles charts, Stevie's second No. 1 single after nearly a decade, and remained there for sixteen weeks.

"Superstition," along with "You Are the Sunshine of My Life," was included in the album "Talking Book," which was released late in 1972. His second one-man album, in which he made heavy use of the synthesizer, it revealed that Stevie was still growing, still refining his music. Critics compared it to a painting, calling it a colorful sonic canvas—which must have struck Stevie, who has never seen a painting, never seen color. "You Are the Sunshine of My Life" has been recorded both vocally and instrumentally by many other artists.

Immediately Stevie plunged into preparations for yet another one-man album. Night and day he worked on it, and those around him understood that it was very necessary for him to be involved in his music even more than his usual custom. After being married one and a half years, he and Syreeta Wright were divorced. The children and stable family life he wanted so deeply would not be his for a while. Commenting on the divorce, he said, "We have no negative feelings for each other. I was too young, and I also dug another person. Besides, she's a Leo. A Taurus and a Leo is like two sticks of dynamite."

Seven months later, seven months of intense, concentrated work, "Innervisions" was released. It was, as Stevie put it, his most personal album, and it meant much to him that those who heard it should share, if only briefly, his world in order to understand how those inner visions had come about. For the first and probably the only time, Stevie held a special press preview of the album. While he wished the reporters to hear the entire album, he was most interested in sharing with them his inspiration for one particular cut, "Living for the City," and so he arranged for a special bus tour for the reporters, a tour through New York City. One reporter recalls, "Some of us thought we knew this place, but then not until we were ready to get on the bus did anybody tell us that we were to be blindfolded, because Stevie wanted us to hear what he himself heard when he was doing the album. So we rode around blindfolded for about forty-five minutes before being brought to the studios for the preview. Still in darkness, we listened attentively, realizing the importance of this album to Stevie and his career, also aware that this is the first time we have been invited to audition any of his albums. The stuff played is heavy, and suddenly each succeeding cut sounds better. . . . Then in the stillness of my blindness, I hear a plaintive voice wailing. . . ."

The song was "Living for the City," and visions of
Harlem flashed through the reporters' minds.

A boy is born in hard time Mississippi
Surrounded by four walls that ain't so pretty
His parents give him love and affection
To keep him strong, moving in the right direction
Living just enough for the city.

His father works some days for fourteen hours
And you can bet he barely makes a dollar
His mother goes to scrub the floor for many
And you'd best believe she hardly gets a penny
Living just enough for the city.

The song swept the black public, for it is somehow
so true either of lives at the time, or of lives once
lived, that it is practically a theme song. It became
the basis for sermons in black churches, for clean-up
campaigns in inner cities. Few other songs have been
so quickly and completely accepted by the U.S. black
community at large, or by blacks in other parts of
the world. This is not to say that only blacks related
to the song. Poverty knows no color, and the words
expressed truth for poor whites as well as blacks.
Other cuts on the album appealed to other groups.
In fact, "Innervisions" contained something for
everybody, although all cuts could be related to by
anyone. Probably the song of greatest impact on the
white audience was "All in Love Is Fair," which

Stevie may have written as a result of his and Syreeta's divorce:

All in love is fair,
Love's a crazy game
Two people vow to stay
But all is changed with time
The future none can see

The road you leave behind
Ahead lies mystery
But all is fair in love
I had to go away
A writer takes his pen
To write the words again
That all in love is fair.

Both Barbra Streisand and Frank Sinatra recorded this song and made solid hits of it. Other cuts on the album that have become popular in their own right are "Don't You Worry 'Bout a Thing," "Visions," and "Higher Ground," a tune that begins in gloom and ends on a joyous note of religious positiveness.

In a sense, Stevie took a big chance when he recorded and released "Innervisions." For he was exposing himself more than most entertainers care to do. He was revealing many of his own deepest thoughts and emotions. Had the critics panned the album, or had the public not bought it, the hurt would have been a much more personal one. But the intensely personal character of the songs is precisely why it has been so successful. Besides being masterfully done in terms of instrumentation and composition, the songs are obviously written and sung from the heart. No false emotion here; it is all quite real.

Real, too, was his exuberance in live performances. One reason why Stevie became one of the most sought-after concert artists in the music world was his ability to establish an instant rapport with his audiences, who recognized immediately that he enjoyed them and enjoyed performing for them. Up on stage, he bounced from piano to drums to synthesizer to harmonica; he danced with the girls of Wonderlove; he threw his head back and sang his heart out. Seeing how much he enjoyed himself, the audience enjoyed themselves.

Stevie lived a life of total immersion in sound. His energy was boundless. "There was a time," Stevie's publicist, personal aide, and "main man" Ira Tucker recalls, "when if he wasn't playing the piano or singing or listening to tapes, he'd get restless and have to go out and do something, buy this or that, or go to the studio . . . something. He never used to sleep. He'd call me at four in the morning and say, 'Hey, we gotta go to the studio, right now.'" He talked incessantly. The bedroom of his New York apartment contained a telephone installation as complicated as that of many businesses, and Stevie liked nothing better than to carry on six conversations at once, switching back and forth from one line to another.

Like any other music star, Stevie had a fairly large entourage: the three girls who made up his back-up singing group, Wonderlove, his band, press agent, personal aides, and the usual hangers-on, the "groupies," as they are called in the business. Some stars welcome everyone, the more the merrier; others cannot stand having so many people around and have frequent tantrums about the situation. Stevie was, and to a certain extent still is, one of the former. Particularly in those first years of freedom from Motown, he was constantly surrounded by people. In Stevie's world, however, it is voices and sounds that surround, and he needed the constant stimulation of sound. Even in a crowded room where the average person could hear merely a babble of voices, Stevie's sensitive hearing could isolate a single conversation. He enjoyed amazing the talkers in question later by repeating their conversation to them. At other times, he enjoyed generalizing yet particularizing his listening. He would organize the various conversations as he would the tracks of sound in his recordings, so that each was a distinct entity and yet part of the over-all whole.

He welcomed sound—any kind of sound—from anywhere. Tunes filled his head to bursting, and sometimes it seemed as if he were racing with his mind in a contest to see if he could get down the ideas in rough form on tape as fast as they came in and left his thoughts.

When he was not living his world of sound while awake, he was doing so while asleep. Just as the sighted dream dreams that correspond to the reality of their waking lives in terms of the senses that come into play, so do the blind. There are no visual images in the dreams of the blind. Instead, there are audio and tactile images, and Stevie Wonder's dreams were as full of audio images as his waking hours, fuller in fact. "Let me tell you something," he will say, "—oh, this is horrible—some of the heaviest tunes I ever wrote will never be heard because they came in a dream. Do you know how horrible that is? In my dream I can get a band together and everything, and ohhhh, it sounds so good, I'm seeing it and everything, and then when I wake up it's all forgotten."

On August 6, 1973, Stevie went into a sleep from which he might well never have awakened. He was riding in a car driven by his cousin, John Harris. They were on the way from Greenville, South Carolina, to Raleigh. Ahead of them was a logging truck, weaving from side to side, and Harris decided to pass it. As Harris started to pull out around the truck suddenly the driver stepped on his brakes, the logs jarred free, and one of them crashed through the windshield and against Stevie's skull.

He lay in a coma in the hospital for three days. "I remember when I got to the hospital in Winston-

Salem," says Ira Tucker, "man, I couldn't even recognize him. His head was swollen up about five times normal size. And nobody could get through to him. I knew that he likes to listen to music really loud and I thought maybe if I shouted in his ear it might reach him. The doctor told me to go ahead and try, it couldn't hurt. The first time I didn't get any response, but the next day I went back and I got right down in his ear and sang "Higher Ground":

I'm so glad he let me try it again
'Cause my last time on earth
I lived a whole world of sin
I'm so glad I know more than I knew then
Gonna keep on tryin'
Till I reach the highest ground. . . .

"His hand was resting on my arm," says Tucker, "and after a while his fingers started going in tune with the song. I said, yeah! Yeeaah! This dude is gonna make it!"

After that Stevie was still in a semi-coma for seven more days. When he finally came out of it, and into full consciousness, he discovered that he had lost his sense of smell. To the average person this loss would not be particularly serious, but to Stevie, who already lacked one major sense, it was devastating. But he worried less about having lost his sense of smell than about another possible loss. He was terrified that he had lost his ability to make music.

"After he came out of the coma," Ira Tucker later

recalled, "we brought one of his instruments—I
think it was the clavinet—to the hospital. For a while,
Stevie just sat there. Didn't do anything with it.
You could see he was afraid to touch it, because he
didn't know if he still had it in him—he didn't know
if he could still play. And then when he finally did
touch it! Man, you could just see the happiness
spreading all over him. I'll never forget that."

It would be some time, however, before Stevie would
do much playing. The brain injury he had suffered
required him to be hospitalized for several weeks and
to spend some two months after that recuperating.
Gradually his sense of smell returned, which relieved
him of some worry. But the months of bed rest and
restricted movement were among the hardest times he
has ever been through. Sighted people have little idea
of how much energy they expend through the use of
their eyes. As mentioned before, lack of this outlet
for excess energy is the source of so-called "blindisms"
in the blind. But Stevie's bodily movements were
also restricted, and for some time he was heavily
tranquilized to ensure quiet. All this produced great
tension in him, until he started to learn how to relax
by using his memory and by turning more closely
than ever to religion.

Just as the blind learn to develop their sense of
hearing, so too they learn to develop their memory.
It is as essential to do this as it is to develop hearing.
The blind must rely on their memory to tell them

With the wounds from his accident in August 1973 still very apparent, Stevie is shown here with his mother, Mrs. Lula Hardaway. The necessary period of recuperation following the accident enabled Stevie to spend more time with her. UNITED PRESS INTERNATIONAL PHOTO

many things that their eyes cannot see. Memorizing is required of a blind person to a much larger extent than of others. Deprived of the stimulation of sight, blind people are more oriented to their own inner world and their minds are constantly preoccupied with going over past experiences. This constant inward looking, like any other practicing, makes their memory excellent. It also causes them to develop a rich fantasy life. Some blind people come to rely on this fantasy life so strongly that they fail to relate to the real world. This did not happen to Stevie. But his ability to look inward and remember helped to get him through those months of convalescence, and when he was again able to be active it provided him with a huge store of song ideas.

He found rest, too, in religion. While the religious implications of Stevie's brush with death have been called corny by some, it is quite likely that those who label it so have never been as close to death as Stevie was. Stevie is convinced that God came to him at the time of the accident, and during his convalescence he had ample time to ponder that event. A brush with death also reminds one of the preciousness of life, and Stevie spent much time after the accident thinking about himself and his place in the world.

One morning, about six weeks after Stevie got out of the hospital, he called Ira Tucker. "Tuck," he said, "when I was out cold in the hospital, did I do a lot of heavy breathing?" "Yeah, man, you sure did," Tucker answered. "I thought so," said Stevie, and hung up. It was very important to Stevie to understand exactly what had happened, exactly how he had been during those lost moments when, though he was living, he was not conscious of it.

4
Stevie Wonder Expanding

Six weeks after his release from the hospital, Stevie was still on medication but able to travel, and when an invitation came to attend an Elton John concert in Boston, he happily accepted. Elton had never met Stevie and did not know that his friends had invited Stevie to the concert. Nor did he know that Stevie would be on his private plane when it left New York for Boston. His promotion people had thought it would be fun to sneak Stevie onto the plane and to have him pose as the cocktail organist.

As expected, Elton was happily surprised, and the two talked for a while as the plane made its way to Boston. At Boston Garden, Stevie accompanied Elton John backstage, where he felt Elton's famous light-up eyeglasses that spelled "Elton." Then he listened happily to an exciting Elton John concert.

When the scheduled concert was over, the audience wanted more, so Elton John did an encore. Then he paused for a moment. "A friend of mine is here," he announced to the audience of eighteen thousand people. "He was badly hurt in an accident some time ago—" He did not have to finish. Instantly the audience knew who he was talking about. They began to applaud, and then some stood, and then the entire huge hallful of people were standing and cheering for Stevie Wonder. He and Elton did "Honky Tonk Woman" together, then Elton stepped back and Stevie, in his first performance since the accident, launched into "Superstition." When Ira Tucker led Stevie down off the stage, it seemed that the building would crumble from the thunder of applause. Later Elton John admitted, "I guess I thought I was the only one totally immersed in music until I met Stevie."

Not long after the Boston Garden concert, Stevie went back to work in earnest. Only now it was a calmer Stevie Wonder who commanded the rented recording studios in New York. He still worked until 2 A.M. at times, but it was no longer with the sense of urgency that says, "Keep going! Time is running out!" Now Stevie Wonder felt secure about time. After all, he reasons, if he had been meant to have a brief career, the accident would have been the end of it. He had ideas for a fourth one-man album, but he felt there was time to do that and other things as well. One "other thing" he did was to produce a second album for his former wife, Syreeta, "Stevie Wonder Presents Syreeta."

During the winter of 1973–74, Stevie did concerts in England, among other countries, and one thing that his staff realized hadn't changed as a result of the accident was his lateness. If anything, due to his new security about having the time to do what he wanted, his tardiness had become worse. Road manager Ira Tucker sighs, "One thing you can depend on with Stevie is that he'll always be late. That's his way of doing things. When we were in England last year, it took Steve three days to get on a plane and leave London. Each day we were supposed to split and each day Steve just couldn't get it together enough to pack. But you just have to go with it."

In March 1974 Stevie Wonder made history. He had already made history of a sort in January, when he had been nominated for six Grammy awards, more than any other recording artist in the sixteen-year history of the awards. But in March the awards were actually given, and it is no exaggeration to say that Stevie stole the show. To begin with, he won five of the six awards for which he had been nominated. These included Album of the Year ("Innervisions"), Best Engineered Recording ("Superstition"), Best Pop Vocal Performance ("Superstition"), Best Rhythm and Blues Single ("Superstition"), and Best Pop Vocal Performance by a Male Singer ("You Are the Sunshine of My Life"). He only accepted four of

91

*With fellow Grammy winners Helen Reddy and Alice Cooper,
Stevie displays one of the five Grammy awards he won for
1973.* WARTOKE CONCERN, INC.

them; the fifth, Best Engineered Recording, he gave
to his engineer!

It was a joyous night for Stevie, but winning the
awards was not as important to him as knowing who
was there to hear, with him, his name announced,
and to watch him being led to the stage five separate
times to accept his awards. His mother was there, and

that meant more than anything else in the world
to the man who, as a little boy, had felt compelled to
reassure her that he didn't mind at all being blind.

Stevie won other awards that year, but they did
not mean as much as the Grammys, the Oscars of the
music business. "Never did I think I would receive a
Grammy," Stevie reflected later. "My only goal and
dream was to touch and know how a Grammy looked.
I guess God didn't let me just touch one. He let me
touch four." In fact, he really was quite displeased
about three of his other awards. The National
Association of Recording Merchandisers named him
best-selling male soul artist of the year, and he received
the American Music awards for best male soul vocalist
and soul single ("Superstition").

"I kinda feel," he sighs, "that after writing all those
songs like 'All in Love Is Fair' and 'Visions,' well,
that to say I'm just a soul artist is wrong because all
those songs are typical ballads of America. I am a
black man but music is music. I want to be an inspiration to my people, but I don't want to be
categorized."

Categorizing is one of Stevie's particular dislikes.
"People are always labeling you," he explains, ". . . as
a performer . . . rather than listening to whatever
it is you're doing and . . . accepting you for what
you are. I mean they're always trying to *comprehend*
you, you see, and they think that by saying, hey, I got
that cat's *label*—you understand?—that they have you

93

all figured out. You can say . . . well *this* dude here is obviously a rock singer . . . or this cat here is a country-western thing . . . you know? So now I know what he *is*, I know *all about him!* . . . It gets to be a ridiculous situation when I come out with a record and some people will say . . . my, my! . . . that doesn't *sound* like Stevie Wonder. . . . How can I not sound like me? That's not my problem, when that happens. That's the problem of somebody who has—ah—jumped to conclusions too quickly."

In late March 1974, Stevie gave his first American concert since the accident at New York's Madison Square Garden. He now sported a mustache, but not to cover any scars resulting from the accident. His scars were quite visible on his forehead. He walked out onto the stage, pointed toward heaven and then to his forehead, and finally gave the audience a huge smile. The garden exploded. He had not said a word, but the audience knew exactly what he was saying to them. By the grace of God, I am back, and this will be an evening of love and joy that you will never forget. He sang both new and old material, including some of his most famous hits. At the end he brought out Sly Stone, Eddie Kendricks, and Roberta Flack to do "Superstition" with him in a rollicking, hand-clapping finale.

Stevie's fourth one-man album, "Fulfillingness' First Finale," was released in the summer of 1974, and by September it was the nation's best-selling LP.

It showed clearly in some parts that something very important had happened to Stevie since he had recorded his last album. A mixture of styles and feelings, it contained the hit single, "You Haven't Done Nothin'," which is perhaps his most "militant" song to date. Beginning with the cynical:

We are amazed but not amused
By all the things you say that you'll do

and containing the refrain:

But we are sick and tired of hearing your song
Tellin' how you are gonna change right from wrong—
'Cause if you really want to hear our views
"You haven't done nothin!"

it expressed impatience with liberals who promise much but deliver little. Some observers feel that Stevie's accident caused him to rethink his position as a black man and to decide that it was worth the risk to express his feelings about the racial situation. But the truth may simply be that, having reached a position of great popularity, Stevie felt secure enough to speak out. Major athletic figures like Bill Russell and Kareem Jabbar waited to speak out until they had reached a position from which they could speak and know their words would mean something.

On the same album is a very religious song, "Heaven Is Ten Zillion Light Years Away," and there is little question that Stevie's religious faith increased as a result of the accident. There are also many songs

Roberta Flack, Sly Stone, and Eddie Kendricks joined Stevie and Wonderlove in a rollicking, hand-clapping rendition of "Superstition" to end Stevie's first American concert after his

accident. It was a show the audience at Madison Square Garden in New York would never forget. PHOTO BY BOB GRUEN, WARTOKE CONCERN, INC.

about love, which has caused some critics to call the album "too gushy" and "too romantic."

But while the album's lyrics seem to have been affected by the accident, it is dangerous to read too much into them. Stevie had written most of the songs before the accident. "I like pretty songs," Stevie explains. "Pretty tunes are coming back, tunes that are melodic but not too melodic, tunes with melodies that stick with you."

Musically, "Fulfillingness' First Finale" was like a gigantic display of his many talents. Here, too, it was possible to see the effects of the accident. During his recuperation, Stevie had spent much time thinking about his growing up years, and his more formal music training showed up undisguised here, especially in the cut "They Won't Go When I Go," which sounded almost like an exercise in Bach and Chopin. He continued and refined his long-held talent for incorporating rhythmic and memorable "riffs" such as the "Doo doo wop" refrain in "You Haven't Done Nothin'." And his musical texturing approached perfection in "It Ain't No Use" in which, with the help of the synthesizer, he incorporated various instrumental tracks, background vocalizing by Wonderlove, background vocalizing by the Persuasions, and his own voice into a harmonious, many-layered composition.

This album, too, contained "something for everyone," lyrically and, particularly, musically. "You Haven't Done Nothin'" was a *now* song; but for the classical music-minded there was "They Won't Go When I Go," from which he switched to the smooth, bossa nova beat of "Bird of Beauty." He reveled in the versatility of his music and of his voice, which ranged from a blues wail to a soft calypso-croon to a Louis Armstrong-growl.

Altogether it was a very self-assured album, quieter and more meditative just as he had become more self-assured, quieter and more meditative since the accident. Stevie had come to understand, as he said in "Bird of Beauty" on the "Fulfillingness'" album, that sometimes "your mind is requesting a vacation." He was able, now, to allow his mind to rest. In fact, he forced it to do so. When he was on tour, for example, he would ask to be taken to a quiet, secluded park in whatever city or town where he was scheduled to appear. He would spend about forty-five minutes in the park, away from the pressures of schedules and booking dates, away from the babble of voices that constantly surrounded him, away from the reporters who wanted to interview him, the promoters who wanted him to appear at this or that benefit. In the park, he would listen to the birds and the children of the city, hear the sounds of the city and understand its character, and when he left he would be ready to go back to the pressures and din of the life of a music star.

Stevie's staff did not particularly mind those park visits of his. At least they always knew where he was, and as the visits usually took place in the afternoons, his absence rarely came dangerously close to a scheduled concert time. Anyway, he could be late for a concert even if he was in his dressing room several hours ahead of time.

"When we were playing Detroit on this last tour," Tucker recalled late in the spring of 1975, "Steve was forty minutes late in going on or something. Everybody's going crazy, you know, having heart attacks because Steve is just sitting in the dressing room trying to get his hair to look right. But I wasn't worried. I said listen, folks, there's no problem here; no reason to panic. After all, Steve was *in* the place; eventually he'd go on and then everything's cool. Then a couple of weeks later we're in Seattle . . . and Steve is due to go on in thirty minutes, the only hangup being that nobody's seen Steve since the day before. Suddenly, as the tension mounts, the phone rings. Guess who? Steve! He was calling from L.A. to say he missed the plane. Missed the *plane*. And he's supposed to be onstage in *thirty minutes.*

"Man," Tucker continued, "that one just blew a lot of people away. And I said, okay . . . *now* we have a problem. *Now* anybody who wants to panic can go right ahead. . . . That, is life with Steve."

Other friends bring up the fact that he doesn't keep regular hours, that he plays his instruments all night, eats when he wants, sleeps when he wants. They insist that Stevie is not purposely being rude or lax in being late; "he just doesn't have days or nights, and he's seldom thinking more than ten minutes ahead." This may be so, but it does not present much consolation for the promoters of concerts or to Stevie's own harried staff. And there is evidence from Stevie himself that his lateness is not uncorrectable. He has said that if he could get an auditorium dancing the way Sly Stone does he would never be late for a concert in his life.

There were other ways in which Stevie showed his independence on this tour. He explains, "I thought instead of just going out and doing *all* Stevie Wonder's Greatest Hits and everything, I'd do some songs that I'd encountered along the way, and that I admire very much. So I did 'Earth Angel,' the Penguin thing, and some Temptations stuff . . . 'Ain't Too Proud to Beg' . . . and 'I Heard It Through the Grapevine,' 'What'd I Say' and just a lot of tunes that I really liked. . . . Then I finished up with 'Fingertips.' "

Immediately some observers again began to predict that Stevie had lost his magic, his creativity. Stevie recalls, "People were saying . . . oh, goodness, that boy's all washed out. They said I was *lowering* myself because I was doing all this. . . . Now, *I* was enjoying myself . . . and the audiences, they were enjoying *themselves* . . . and yet people seemed to take this as a sign that I was never going to do anything worthwhile again, which is stupid, naturally."

At the 1973 Grammy awards presentations, Stevie shared his joy with fiancée Yolanda Simmons. WILLIAM R. EASTABROOK PHOTO

At another time in his life, this reaction might have bothered Stevie greatly. But at that time it did not, particularly, for he had fallen in love with a young woman named Yolanda Simmons. She had joined Stevie's entourage as his secretary-bookkeeper, and in a short time they had fallen in love. Sighted people are often so concerned with physical appearance that they do not take time to find out about the inner person before they fall in love. People who are blind are just as prone to the pitfalls involved in falling in love, and perhaps more so in some cases, as are people who are sighted. They fall in love out of need, out of loneliness, out of selfishness. Stevie knew from personal experience that one can fall in love for many wrong reasons. But he was convinced that he would never fall in love with someone who was not, inside, a beautiful person. "I can usually tell about a woman by her conversation," Stevie says, "her voice and the way she carries herself. Some women can have a very beautiful outer face and a very ugly inner face."

Nor would he fall in love with someone who was not willing to see beyond his stardom to the real person. He recalls, "I used to meet girls and I'd say, 'You know me as Stevie Wonder but I want you to know me like I am. I mean, eventually I'm going to stop singing. . . .' And she'd say, 'No, no, you can't stop singing!' And I'd say, 'But my name is really Steve Morris.' And she'd say, 'Yeah, but you'll always be Little Stevie Wonder to me, baby!' " That is *not* what Stevie wanted in a woman.

Yolanda was different. Certainly she was proud of his talent and pleased with his fame, but she loved Stevie as a person, not as a personality. She radiated the sort of inner beauty that he, perhaps better than sighted people, could identify. Early in 1975 Stevie and Yolanda moved into a Civil War-period brownstone house on East 18th Street in Manhattan, and in April 1975 their daughter was born. They named her Aisha Zakia, combining African words meaning "strength" and "intelligence." "I want to be young with my kids," Stevie has said. "Wow, I really want 'em, boy or girl, doesn't matter, that's part of *you,* the sunshine of your life."

In the fall of 1974, to publicize "Fulfillingness' First Finale" Stevie toured thirty cities. People were eager to see him, to be sure he had recovered from his injuries, and there was great demand for his new music. By October 1974, over 40,000,000 copies of his records had been sold. He had accumulated fourteen gold singles, four gold albums, and two platinum albums (over 1 million copies sold). He had appeared on the cover of *Newsweek* and had been called by some the most creative and most respected entertainer in the business. In March 1975 he added five more Grammys to his collection, accepting one in memory of Elijah Muhammad and Jack Benny. As writer O'Connell Driscoll commented, "Anyone who can stand up on national television and accept a Grammy award in the memory of Elijah Muhammad and Jack Benny can do anything at all."

In August of 1975, the first annual "Rockie" awards ceremony was held. It was the first time rock music and rock entertainers had been recognized for their contributions, and there was an air of self-consciousness about the ceremony, a sense of the necessity of establishing rock music as a separate entity. Stevie was there. He and his work had been

Stevie Wonder performs selections from his fourth one-man album, "Fulfillingness' First Finale," which in the opinion of many is the most complete showcase of his many talents he has yet produced. WARTOKE CONCERN, INC.

nominated for six awards, and unlike many musical celebrities, Stevie considers such awards important enough to be accepted personally. Sitting with Yolanda, he listened to the presentations and the

Singer Bette Midler presents Stevie with the National Academy of Recording Arts and Sciences Grammy for the best male vocalist of 1974. UNITED PRESS INTERNATIONAL PHOTO

interim banter with his head down and cocked slightly to one side. When winners were announced, he clapped rigorously, and his head bobbed back and forth as happily for his fellow entertainers as it would have if he had won the awards himself. Stevie and his work were nominated for three "Rockies." "Fulfillingness' First Finale" was up for best album. Bob Dylan's "Blood on the Tracks" won. He was nominated for outstanding rock star of the year. Elton John won that. He was nominated for the best male vocalist award, and that one he won.

Yolanda led him up the stairs to the stage and then over to the podium. The gold medal was placed around his neck, and the audience broke into applause. Some people stood, but more did not. In accepting the "Rockie," Stevie mentioned Cannonball Adderly, a veteran rhythm and blues performer who had just died. "I'd like to ask you a favor," said Stevie. "Just stand until I get back down offstage, in memory of Cannonball Adderly. Mercy. Mercy. Mercy." He did not know that most were not standing when he made his request. He did hear scattered applause when there should have been silence, as if some members of the audience had not been listening when he made his request. To Stevie Wonder fans, the incident seemed somewhat insulting, but it should be pointed out that this, the first awards presentation for rock music, was charged with excitement and that the audience was restless.

Stevie Wonder had won several Grammys as well as numerous other awards, including five Ebony awards in the rhythm and blues category a few days earlier. He was pleased that his music was recognized and honored in diverse musical fields.

Stevie does not like labeling. "I don't like it when one is put into a category of music," he says, "so that when he ventures into some other kind of music the press or the public has a hard time relating to it. It seems that every person is put into a certain bag. Being an artist is not being limited to one kind of music. For instance, soul music was derived from gospel and early rhythm and blues. In my mind, soul means feeling. When a person is categorized as a soul artist because of his color, I don't like it. True artistry is about variety, the real spice of an artist's life.

"I have never been labeled in my own mind," says Stevie. Now, no one else labels him either. One of the most popular stars in the music business, Stevie is what is known in the business as a "monster," a star who can automatically fill any auditorium or arena and whose records appeal to every audience category. Since he won his five Grammys in 1974, he has been of interest to every observer of the national scene. Articles on him have appeared in all the major news magazines and music magazines, as well as in a variety of other publications. Things that he does or things about him that would have gone unnoticed in 1972 or 1973 are newsworthy items now. The contract he signed with Motown in August of 1975, however, would have been news at any time. The two-year, thirteen-million-dollar contract was the largest ever made with a recording star. But Motown expected to get more than that back, beginning with its share of the profits from Stevie's first double album, which was released in 1976.

There are others who would like to share in Stevie's success, and another result of his fame, with which he has had to learn to live, is being constantly besieged by promoters, con artists, and a variety of other people, each with his or her own particular "hype" designed to exploit him for financial purposes. Stevie has become very skilled at imitating such people:

White hustler: "Steve . . . seriously Steve . . . on the real side . . . I want to manage you. I mean, Steve, what are you doing playing these places . . . the Fillmore? Steve, I can get you into the *Copa*."

Black hustler: "See now, bro', we got this *thang* we tryin' to get together, this *benefit* thang down here, and we need you to come on down and do your thang for us here, bro', you dig? 'Cause I know you can dig this, brotha, we tryin' to get this money so we can funnel it *back into the community,* you dig?"

In addition to making him a prime target for all sorts of hustlers, Stevie's fame has also caused him to become a symbol. While he is pleased to have achieved such renown, at the same time he feels that in seizing upon him as the vanguard of the new (black) music the media are being too simplistic in their approach, "missing the point," as Stevie puts it. "They're going on about me," he says, "saying how I'm this and that and now I'm a superstar. . . . It was like . . . I mean it was as if they *decided* that black music was the thing that was going on *now*. It was as if they looked around and said . . . hey! there's black music going on! And then . . . they had to go find some black cat who . . . They're looking for a *symbol* of all this that they think is going on."

Symbols, while often overpraised, are also open to unfair criticism. Many observers and writers are naturally suspicious of a star with as few known faults or weaknesses as Stevie seems to have, and when they do suspect a fault or weakness they emphasize it out of proportion. Those who have called Stevie a "washout" when he has chosen to sing the songs of others jumped to their negative conclusions much too quickly. Naturally Stevie is as disturbed by what he considers unfair criticism as he is bothered by overpraise. But he tries not to take to heart what is written or said about him. Many famous people insist on reviewing whenever possible what is written about them before it is released. Stevie feels that if someone is going to "do a job on him," it will be done no matter what he says.

"Obviously, you don't get the opportunity to perform if people don't know who you are," says Stevie about his fame. "But when you start to believe the things you read about yourself . . . like when you begin thinking that you really *are* number one . . . that's when you begin to go nowhere. I mean if there really was such a thing as *number one,* well then whoever that lucky cat was would have no place left to go. You see?"

Success has definitely not spoiled Stevie Wonder. "I'm still basically me," he says. "I'm a happy guy who believes that no matter how big an artist becomes, he should still treat everyone on the same level. I don't want to be God and I'm not going to be a beast, either. The only people who are really blind are those whose eyes are so obscured by hatred and bigotry that they can't see the light of love and justice. As for me, I would like to see the world, the earth, the birds and grass—but my main concern is with self-expression, with giving a part of the gift God gave to me: my music."

The most important result of his success, in Stevie's opinion, is the opportunity it gives him to lead a life of total immersion in sound. It enables him to buy expensive radios and recording equipment, but more importantly it enables him to afford the luxury of spending twenty-four hours a day, if he wants, enjoying and creating music. He can get so "high" on music that it is easy to see why those who do not

111

Stevie loves to get inside a recording studio with all its marvelous equipment. With the help of the Arp and Moog synthesizers he is able to incorporate various instrumental and vocal tracks into a harmonious, many-layered composition.
WIDE WORLD PHOTOS

know him suspect that he must be on some kind of drugs. But Stevie does not even drink. He used to drink beer and wine at times before the accident, but since the accident he has drunk nothing alcoholic. His favorite drink is apple juice, and he has his own apple juice maker. His relationship with music can literally be called a love affair. In fact, he is much more comfortable with music than he is with people. For all his outward friendliness, he is really rather wary, and he trusts very few people. "Well," Stevie admits, "I distance myself. I remove myself from people, but I don't feel alienated from them. . . . If people want to take the time to listen to my music, they can hear *me,* my way of talking to them."

Part of his wariness is due to the fact that he is black, in a society where despite fame and talent and money a different skin hue is still a liability, still denies equal humanity. Stevie is still troubled by, as he says, "the fact that you have to demand respect as a black man and a black entertainer. Let me say this: I would never go around saying, 'Hey, I *am.*' But so many of us have to demand respect. Do you understand how much noise Muhammad Ali had to make before he was respected? It's ridiculous, it's absurd. At his age—and he is old in the fighting world—he had to prove himself. Those are the things which hurt —me, you."

Part of his wariness is also due, no doubt, to his blindness, for he knows that it makes him more vulnerable. He understands the limitations imposed by his handicap, and with those whom he knows and trusts he feels quite secure about it. He and his staff often joke about it, and quite frequently his staff play tricks on him, such as pretending to be playing a tune on an instrument when they are really playing a tape recording. Stevie continually practices and perfects his hearing. He can hear a faint stomach rumble and know someone is hungry. He can identify the crunching sound of someone eating French bread. Above all, his blindness has given him an opportunity for the other senses and unknown qualities to extend themselves, so the supposed disability becomes less of one, more of an asset. It is almost as if his blindness has given him an edge in the world of sound.

Stevie breaks into song on elevators, in bathrooms, in hallways, anywhere. His staff members always have a cassette tape recorder handy, for neither they nor Stevie ever know when a tune will come to him. It can happen anywhere—in a restaurant or in a bus or car. "Hey, how about this!" Stevie will say. "Doo doo da doo . . . now hold it for four counts . . . pom pom pom . . . yeah, then a C-major seventh, pom pom pompom, C-minor seventh, then a D with a C in the bass. . . ." If it happens in a public place, people will crowd around to listen in awe and respect. Who knows, this tune may be his next hit. Tunes come to him all the time, and he has hundreds stored away on tapes that he hasn't recorded or even refined.

The sources for his song ideas are as varied as the ideas themselves. "I listen to a lot of people," Stevie explains. "I hear a phrase, a certain riff; this is how we all come up with ideas. It's the same thing as reading somebody's poem or learning somebody else's steps."

114

A new song may be born in a short riff, or just a few notes. "Usually what happens," Stevie explains, "is that the melody comes first and then sometime later I'll write the lyrics. If I have my tape recorder on my piano I'll put it down on the cassette, just the melody. If I'm in the studio and I come up with something spontaneously, I'll just put down the rhythm track, which consists usually of the Moog programmed for the bass part, and the piano or clavinet or whatever I'm using. Then later I'll add the other instruments, the horns and strings and all. When the song is almost complete, that's when I'll lay down the true lyrics. It's the last thing but I will have been thinking about lyrics all along. I'll maybe come up with a punch line and then work around that theme . . . certain weeks you can write and then the next week you can't do nothin'. It's an involuntary movement. But you can't be getting worried when it doesn't come."

It might seem to some to be a frivolous life, like that of a child playing with an endless array of toys. But it just happens that what Stevie enjoys most, what is most important in his life, is also that which gives purpose to his life and through which he feels he can make his most meaningful contribution—music.

"I want to make it clear to you," Stevie says, "that I take what I do very seriously; and since my accident, I suppose I take it even *more* seriously. Because from that point on I realized that I was just lucky to be *alive* . . . and it became very clear to me that it wasn't enough *just* to be a rock and roll singer or anything of that nature. I had to make *use* of whatever talent I have. So when I get on a stage and perform I'm *saying* something to people; and I'm saying it in the way that's most effective for me. . . . When an audience comes to hear me perform, they know I'm not going to put them to sleep with my moral indignation, dig it? They know I'm going to do a show, which is why they came. So I give them their show; I entertain them—because I *am* an entertainer, regardless of what a lot of people think: I'm not a politician or a minister—but at the same time I can . . . ah . . . *enlighten* them a little."

Stevie is strongly committed to racial equality and social justice. He does countless benefit concerts every year, and frequently donates money to various charities, including his entire earnings from his second Madison Square Garden concert, which took place about a year after his first at the Garden. He made a guest appearance on a "One-to-One" telethon to ask the public to support it, and ended up giving ten thousand dollars himself. He is very interested in the work of the Louis Braille Foundation for Blind Musicians. He is extremely modest about his benefit work and often expresses concern that his own appearance will detract from the cause itself. In recent years Stevie has become very much interested in Africa, which is natural for a young black man. He

Stevie does a duet with one of the Muppets of "Sesame Street."
Stevie has a special interest in children and makes a point of
being available for as many activities for children as he can.

yearns to learn about his heritage, to commune with it
in his unique, non-visual way. He also wants to help
the people of Africa, particularly those people who
have been hit by severe drought or blinded by a fungus-
carrying fly that feeds on the cornea.

"I understand there are many flies in that part of

Africa. And when a child is born, they'll try to settle in the corner of the eye and eat on the cornea. And as a result, the children grow blind. So I want to raise money here and use it to eradicate this fly problem.

"I don't know how long I'll be there," he says of his trip to Africa, planned tentatively for sometime in 1977, "but it'll take me about two years to raise the money I'll need, and to find a place to stay there. Plus, when I go, I want to tour several countries of Africa."

Reactions to his plans have not pleased Stevie. In fact, he gets by turn angry and sad when he thinks about it. "There are three things that irk me now," he says. "There are those people who are saying I'm playing Robin Hood, taking money from the blacks here (America) and giving it to the poor blacks there (Africa), and those Africans who don't want black artists over there using the drought and many other things as an excuse to rip off the country.

"I really feel very very bad that people would actually think that I would be so cruel to take money from here and take it over there. I've got an obligation to my people here as well as there. That's why a lot of my money is going to stay in this country and help my people here. . . . But any time one group of people feels that the other has any more, that group immediately comes down with some jive like: 'Steve ain't goin' do nothin' for us. He done forgot all about us. He's going to take all of what we gave him and give it to the boys over there.' It's unfortunate that this world is like this."

Helping the victims of drought and blindness is a very ambitious project, but Stevie Wonder has undertaken and succeeded in a variety of ambitious tasks in his comparatively short lifetime. He has adjusted to and in many ways conquered the handicap of his blindness; he has been in a bizarre accident, come close to death, and emerged with a new sense of purpose and inner peace. He has done battle with a giant corporation and won, has bucked the music business "system," has succeeded in the tremendously costly and complex task of producing his own albums. Most important of all, in his opinion, is his achievement of freedom—something that as a blind person, and particularly as a black person, has not been easy to win.

He remembers the time when he was the only black kid on the school bus and was ashamed to be heard listening to B.B. King on his transistor radio. "Freedom begins in the simplest things," he says, "even in such things as feeling free enough to turn on a radio to a particular station. You have to seize that for yourself. . . ."

It is sentiments like these that Stevie Wonder expresses, and hopes will be heard, in his music, his "gift from God." This is the source of the most frequent criticism of his music: corny . . . too sentimental . . . lacks 1970s sophistication. His songs talk about love, humanity, justice, about his vision of love and respect between people regardless of economic and social class, regardless of the color of their skin. All this has been said before, and it seems boring to many in a highly politicized generation that prizes independence, "doing one's own thing," "finding oneself," and cynicism. As one writer put it, "I couldn't help wishing that his philanthropy had some political content and that he didn't sound quite so much like a 1963 brotherhood speech." But as the same writer admitted, the values and emotions of which Stevie Wonder sings are as important to us now and we yearn for them as much as ever. That is why we have made him a star.

Discography

Albums in Print

Songs in the Key of Life
Fulfillingness' First Finale—Gold
In Loving Memory
Innervisions—Gold
Motown Christmas
Motown Story
Music of My Mind—Gold
Recorded Live at Newport in New York
Talking Book—Gold
Stevie Wonder's Greatest Hits, Vol. I
Stevie Wonder's Greatest Hits, Vol. II

Singles in Print

Bedtime for Toys
Big Brother

Blame It on the Sun
Blowin' in the Wind
Boogie on Reggae Woman
Castles in the Sand
Don't You Worry 'Bout a Thing
Evil
Fingertips (2 Parts)—Gold
For Once in My Life—Gold
Heaven Help Us All—Gold
Hey Love
Higher Ground—Gold
I Call It Pretty Music (2 Parts)
I Was Made to Love Her—Gold
If You Really Love Me—Gold
I'm Wondering
Keep Running
Living for the City—Gold
My Cherie Amour—Gold
Nothing's Too Good for My Baby
Place in the Sun
Seems So Long
Sho-Be-Doo-Be-Do-Da-Day
Signed, Sealed and Delivered—Gold
Superstition—Gold
Superwoman—Gold
Think of Me as Your Soldier
Uptight (Everything's All Right)—Gold

Visions
We Can Work It Out
What Christmas Means to Me
With a Child's Heart
Yester Me, Yester You, Yesterday—Gold
You Are the Sunshine of My Life—Gold
You Haven't Done Nothin'
You Met Your Match

Index

Italics indicate illustration